HAPPY AND GLORIOUS

HAPPY AND GLORIOUS

THE REVOLUTION OF 1688

MICHAEL I. WILSON

Front cover illustration: William and Mary presenting the Cap of Liberty to Europe, by Sir James Thornhill. Detail from the ceiling of the Painted Hall at the Old Royal Naval College, Greenwich. (© ORNC and Jigsaw Design & Publishing, 2010.)

Back cover: The Burning of HMS *Royal James* at the Battle of Solebay, by Willem van de Velde the Younger. (© National Maritime Museum, Greenwich, London.)

First published 2014

The History Press
The Mill, Brimscombe Port
Stroud, Gloucestershire, GL5 2QG
www.thehistorypress.co.uk

British Library Cataloguing in Publication Data.
A catalogue record for this book is available from the British Library.

ISBN 978 0 7524 6182 3

Typesetting and origination by The History Press
Printed in Great Britain

CONTENTS

FOREWORD

After a promising start to his reign early in 1685 King James II turned out to be dictatorial, devious, and intent on getting his own way in everything. He believed firmly in his Divine Right to rule, and as a fanatical Catholic he wanted above all to reinstate his own faith as the official religion of the nation. As for Parliament, to him it was simply an irritation, little more than a supply depot to which he was obliged to go whenever he needed money. The Glorious Revolution of 1688/89 changed all this. It was a milestone in the progress towards Parliamentary democracy in Britain, and its outcome was far-reaching. The principle of the Divine Right of Kings, the cause of so much trouble under all the Stuart monarchs, was finally discredited. For the first time in the history of these islands the reigning monarch became answerable to Parliament over a wide spectrum of policies. No longer could he (or she) embark unchecked on expensive foreign adventures or wage unpopular wars. No longer could he try to impose religious beliefs on his people, or interfere with the work of the judiciary. No longer could he set up a standing army with personal allegiance to himself. Perhaps even more remarkably, all this and more was achieved without the widespread bloodshed and strife which at one time had seemed inevitable.

Michael Wilson guides us through this momentous period with clarity and precision. I feel sure that his highly readable account will help greatly towards making this somewhat neglected yet immensely significant episode in our island history better known to students and general readers alike.

Jack Straw, 2014

PREFACE AND ACKNOWLEDGEMENTS

Three hundred years ago the Stuart monarchy came to an end with the death of Queen Anne on 1 August 1714. Yet it could so easily have ended sooner, amidst the violence and bloodshed of a civil war. Instead events took a different course, culminating in the 'Glorious Revolution' of 1688–89.

Over the years historians have produced many books and articles about the Revolution, yet to many people it remains something of a mystery. What started it, why was it 'Glorious', and what was it all about anyway? Who were the principal figures involved? In their spoof history book *1066 and All That* (1930), W.C. Sellar and R.J. Yeatman manage in their own inimitable way to sum up the entire episode in a few words, telling us that because of James II's behaviour, 'the people lost control of themselves altogether and … declared that the answer was an Orange.' The accompanying illustration shows an orange topped by a crown and labelled 'Williamanmary'.

There is clearly much more to the Revolution than this – indeed so much more that one reason why the subject often seems so daunting may be the number and complexity of the issues involved, whether religious, political, social or personal. It is the aim of this book to try to simplify these issues and so to make plain both to students and to the general reader the main underlying causes of the Revolution – the seeds of which were sown in the previous reign – as well as charting its progress. It is not the intention either to take sides or to propose new theories, but simply to follow events as they unfolded. In the process it may be that not all the participants have received the attention due to them, and that some lesser events have been omitted. Nevertheless, if at the end of the journey the reader gains a clearer sense of what actually happened and why, the book will have served its purpose.

My thanks are due to the following for permission to quote from material within their copyright: HarperCollins Publishers Ltd (*The Diary of Samuel Pepys* ed. R.C. Latham and W. Matthews), and Batcheller Monkhouse on behalf of the Trustees of the Will of Major Peter Evelyn (*The Diary of John Evelyn* ed. E.S. de Beer). I also thank my publishers, and especially Mark Beynon, for the care they have taken with the production of this book. And I am grateful beyond measure to all those who between them, during the writing process, have freely given me generous portions of their time and patience, moral support and encouragement, and have shared with me much valuable technical expertise and historical knowledge.

WHAT'S IN A NAME?

The political and constitutional upheaval which is the subject of this book is usually known as the Glorious Revolution. How it got this title is less certain, but one explanation has more credibility than most.

In 1689 the political activist John Hampden was summoned to appear before a committee of the House of Lords which was enquiring into the repercussions of the Rye House Plot. There are differing reports of the proceedings, and while one of these links Hampden with the phrase 'this glorious Revolution', the official account of the committee records it as 'this most happy Revolution'. It is not entirely clear from these reports whether Hampden actually used the words himself. Although the first version has become the norm, the second clearly has an equally important claim to recognition and use. Both are therefore reflected in the title of this book, although 'the Glorious Revolution' is the term generally used in the text.

Sources: Journal of the House of Lords, vol. XIV, p. 379; H.C. Foxcroft (ed.), *The Life and Letters of Sir George Savile, Bart., first Marquess of Halifax*, 2 vols, 1898, vol. II, p. 95; information from Adrian Brown, House of Lords Library.

CALENDARS OLD
AND NEW

Although the Gregorian or New Style calendar had been in use throughout most of Western Europe since 1584, the Julian or Old Style version continued to be used in Britain until 1752. In this mode the New Year officially began not on 1 January but on 25 March, the interim period forming the last three months of the previous year instead of the first three of the following year. However, in this book the New Style calendar is applied throughout and 1 January is indeed New Year's Day.

To complicate matters further, British Old Style dates are eleven days behind those of the New Style. Where necessary, this discrepancy is indicated in the text by (OS) or (NS).

WAR ON THE
HIGH SEAS

*I*t was 6 February 1685. In his bedroom overlooking the Thames, in the rambling old Palace of Whitehall, King Charles II lay dying. In common with the other private apartments in the Palace, the room was not grand but quite small and dark; now it was also noticeably stuffy, owing to the crowd of church-men, courtiers, officials and servants who had pressed their way in to witness their king's last hours. With typical irony he begged their collective pardon for taking 'such an unconscionable long time a-dying', and faintly voiced a plea on behalf of his best-known mistress Nell Gwynn which today is no less poignant for being so familiar –'don't let poor Nelly starve!'

Four days earlier, on 2 February, Charles had been unexpectedly laid low by a stroke. He had already suffered one in 1681 which, while not incapacitating him, had certainly taken its toll. From then onwards he spent more time away from London, mainly at Newmarket or Windsor, enjoying hawking, racing and theatricals. His relationships with his various mistresses grew less tempestuous, and he became absorbed in new building projects at Whitehall, Greenwich and Winchester. However, at New Year 1685 there was no sign of any impending crisis. Indeed, on the evening of Sunday 25 January the diarist John Evelyn, on a visit to Whitehall, was scandalised to find the king publicly toying with no less than three of his mistresses (Barbara Palmer, Duchess of Cleveland, Louise de Kéroualle, Duchess of Portsmouth, and Hortense Mancini, Duchess of Mazarin), whilst around him his roistering courtiers gambled away huge sums of money.[1]

And now, for the pleasure-loving, politically devious Charles, such scenes of unashamed debauchery were over. As he lay patiently waiting for death whilst enduring the various drastic treatments prescribed by his doctors, his queen – the Portuguese Catherine of Braganza, originally a neglected and slightly pathetic figure – sent word that she was too upset to visit him and asking his forgiveness for anything she might have done in the past to distress or offend him. (If ever there was a case of the boot being on the other foot, this was surely it.) In contrast, his brother James, Duke of York and heir to the throne, scarcely left the bedside where he knelt weeping continuously. It could be said that his tears, though certainly genuine, were also prophetic, in view of the distress and misery that he was not only about to suffer himself, but would also inflict upon many of his subjects. Before setting out to trace the steps which led to this sad state of public affairs it may be rewarding, in these first chapters, to consider the main events of James' earlier years, as a means of evaluating his developing character.

He was born on 14 October 1633, the second of Charles I's three sons, and was created Duke of York immediately after baptism. Four years later he was painted by Van Dyck in a group portrait with his brother Charles and his sisters, a solemn child still in petticoats – for at this time boys were not 'breeched' until the age of 5 or 6. His childhood, which was passed mainly in the now vanished palace of Richmond, came to an abrupt end in 1642 with the onset of the Civil War. He accompanied his father Charles I in the early campaigning, and together with the younger Charles received an early baptism of fire at the indecisive Battle of Edgehill.

After Edgehill James went with his father to Oxford, which became the Royalist headquarters and centre of court life for the next four years. The king and his entourage took over Christchurch, whilst Merton was allotted to the queen, Henrietta Maria. Although James may well have benefited from instruction or tutoring from some of the resident academics, the atmosphere of Oxford at that time was hardly conducive to study. Never a large town, Oxford was now filled to bursting point with an influx of courtiers, soldiers, servants and associated hangers-on, supplemented by large numbers of horses and pack-animals in need of extra fodder and stabling. Inevitably such conditions bred disease. The situation was briefly but tellingly described by Lady Anne Fanshawe, then a girl of 18:

> We had the perpetual discourse of losing and gaining towns and men; at the windows the sad spectacle of war, sometimes plague, sometimes sickness of other kinds, by reason of so many people being packed together, as I believe there never was before of that quality; always want; yet I must needs say that most bore it with a martyr-like cheerfulness.[2]

At first, to the young Duke of York life in Oxford no doubt had a *frisson*, an air of suppressed excitement welcome to an active 11-year-old, if less so to the adults around him. Four years later, when his father abandoned the cause and fled to Scotland in May 1646, things looked altogether bleaker to the adolescent James, who now found himself taken back in custody to St James's Palace in London, in the care of the Earl of Northumberland. The conditions were not severe, and James was allowed on several occasions to visit his father at Hampton Court, where the king – having been handed over by the Scots – was now the prisoner of the army. At these meetings (which do not seem to have been very closely monitored), Charles urged James not only to support his brother the younger Charles – now safely in France – but also to do his utmost to try to escape, and to join his mother and brother there. In 1647 James did indeed plot an escape, but a coded letter which he had written was seized and the plot was foiled. No action was taken against him, but he had to promise not to make any other attempts to run away. This promise, like many another still to come, he did not keep.

At St James's Palace he shared his quarters with his brother Henry, Duke of Gloucester, and his younger sister Elizabeth, aged 7 and 13 respectively. On 20 April 1648, whilst playing a game of hide-and-seek with them in the labyrinthine rooms of the Palace, lax security enabled James to make a pre-planned escape into nearby St James's Park, where a Royalist soldier of fortune, Colonel Joseph Bampfield (acting under covert instructions from Charles I), was waiting to spirit him away to a safe house near London Bridge. From here, now convincingly disguised as a girl, James made it down the Thames to Tilbury and thence in a small Dutch ship to the Netherlands, where he was happily received by his elder sister Mary. At the age of 12 Mary had married Prince William of Orange on 2 May 1641 in London, and she had joined her husband at The Hague in the following year.

James was growing up to be a handsome young man. Although ominously obstinate and self-opinionated, he was also brave and resourceful, qualities which stood him in good stead after the execution of his father in January 1649. For four years he moved around Europe – to Paris and St Germain-en-Laye to be with his mother Queen Henrietta Maria, to his sister at The Hague, to Jersey with his brother Charles (who made him governor of the island, a post which he occupied for almost a year), to his aunt Elizabeth, Queen of Bohemia, at Rhenen near Arnhem. On the whole it was not a happy time. There was tension between the new King Charles and their mother Henrietta Maria, and James at first found it difficult to decide to which of them he owed his allegiance. The queen's strong Catholicism was also an issue, although she does not seem to have put direct pressure on James to convert. A political turning point was reached with the defeat of Charles at the Battle of Worcester in the autumn of 1651, following his attempt to regain the English Crown with the help of the Scots, who had already crowned him their own king at Scone. For some time after the battle there was no news of him, but at last he reappeared in France, to the great joy of his family.

But the rejoicings were tempered by gloom and a general sense that the outlook for the Stuarts was now bleak indeed. It seemed they were condemned to be losers, and impoverished ones at that. Prompted by the need to make some money, James sought the permission of his brother and their mother to turn soldier. They agreed, and in 1652 he embarked on a military career, serving first in France in the army of the celebrated Marshal Turenne until 1655. His was no carefully protected behind-the-lines staff post; on the contrary, he saw considerable action and was often in personal danger. His reward was the friendship and admiration of Turenne and promotion to the rank of lieutenant general at the age of 20, the youngest of eight of Turenne's officers to hold that rank.

Political expediency now forced King Charles to move out of France and into Flanders, and to seek the support of the Spanish in helping him to regain his throne. He set up his court first in Bruges and later in Brussels, and in 1656 ordered the Duke of York to join him. James did so with reluctance, and there was further tension between the brothers. An argument over James' choice of a secretary (Sir John Berkeley) was resolved when he was allowed to keep the secretary, provided he himself joined the Spanish army. He did so in 1657, though without much enthusiasm, as he correctly foresaw that this would bring him into actual conflict with his friend and mentor Turenne. This was indeed what happened, especially at the battle which was fought between the French and the Spanish on 14 June 1658 amongst the sand-dunes of Dunkirk. James personally led two cavalry charges, but both failed and he was forced to retreat. Just as before, when he had been with Turenne, he exposed himself recklessly to injury or even death, and it seems that on more than one occasion he was saved only by his stout and serviceable armour. Whatever his faults, he well deserved Sir William Coventry's later description of him (relayed by Samuel Pepys in his *Diary*, 4 June 1664) as 'a man naturally martial to the hottest degree'.

Oliver Cromwell died on 3 September 1658, and news of this event galvanised the exiled court at Brussels, to which James was now attached. Cromwell's successor, his son Richard – known as 'Tumbledown Dick' – had no stomach for the job and resigned his office after a year. However, in the febrile atmosphere of Brussels, plots of invasions launched from France and uprisings encouraged at home came to nothing, and hope was replaced by despondency. Yet, as so often in the course of history, the darkest hour presaged the dawn, and in the later months of 1659 events in England began to move rapidly towards change. Antagonism between the army and the discredited Rump Parliament had reached a pitch that threatened to spill over into anarchy. In Scotland, the general commanding the Parliamentary forces there, George Monck – a strong believer in the supremacy of civil over military power – watched with concern as the Commonwealth unravelled, and decided to take matters into his own hands. On 1 January 1660, as Samuel Pepys sat down to make the first-ever entry in his famous *Diary*, Monck crossed the River Tweed into England at the head of his well-disciplined troops and made his way down to London, where he took immediate and decisive steps to restore the authority of Parliament and so stabilise the volatile situation. At the end of April an official invitation was sent to King Charles from the new Parliament, asking him to return to England and assume the Crown.

A flotilla of ships set out for The Hague to bring the new monarch home. It was headed by the flagship *Naseby*, which carried the admiral in charge of the whole operation. This was Sir Edward Mountagu – a former Cromwellian politician and seafarer who had now convincingly switched sides – and amongst his immediate entourage was his young cousin and confidential secretary Samuel Pepys, not long appointed (13 March) and now relishing his first experience of being at the very centre of important events. For his part in the king's return Mountagu was created Earl of Sandwich and a Knight of the Garter, but although he is always respectfully identified as 'my Lord' in his kinsman's *Diary*, the usage predates his ennoblement. In fact important figures in the Commonwealth were often given the title purely as a matter of courtesy, and Pepys was only following custom.

On 22 May the Duke of York arrived on board the *Naseby* for a visit of inspection, together with his younger brother Henry; they made a handsome and resplendent pair, 'the Duke of York in yellow trimmings, the Duke of Gloucester in grey and red,' reported Pepys. (Sadly, Henry was to die of smallpox only four months later, aged 20.) The Duke of York had already been confirmed in office as Lord High Admiral, a title which had been bestowed on him as a child – despite his tender years – by his father. He returned to England in another ship, the *London*, while the king himself sailed on the *Naseby*, now newly renamed the *Royal Charles*. Charles II landed at Dover on 25 May and entered London on 29 May – his 30th birthday. Samuel Pepys was not on hand to record the pageantry, being still at Dover with the fleet, but his fellow-diarist John Evelyn was there and caught something of the excitement; he saw the king ride into town:

> with a Triumph of above 20,000 horse and foot, brandishing their swords and shouting with unexpressable joy; the ways straw'd with flowers, the

bells ringing, the streets hung with tapestry, fountains running with wine ... the windows and balconies all set with ladies, trumpets, music, and myriads of people flocking the streets and was as far as Rochester, so as they were 7 hours in passing the City ... I stood in the Strand, and beheld it, and blessed God.

Riding near his brother in the procession, the Duke of York was probably no less elated. Conscious too of his position as Lord High Admiral, it was not long before he began to assert his authority in this new role. The navy which Charles II inherited from the failed Commonwealth experiment was large and well equipped, yet not so good that it could not be further improved, and the Lord High Admiral took a close interest in these developments.

By early July 1660 he had already set out his ideas on the shape of naval administration, in particular the setting up of a seven-man Navy Board, of whom the most active, efficient and energetic was the Clerk of the Acts (i.e. secretary), Samuel Pepys, now appointed at the strikingly youthful age of 27. The appointment was made at the suggestion of Lord Sandwich, and the duke soon realised that in Pepys he had got a bargain; he congratulated the earl, who passed on the good news: 'He did tell me how much I was beholding to the Duke of York, who did yesterday of his own accord ... thank him for one person brought into the Navy, naming myself, and much more to my commendation, which is the greatest comfort and encouragement that ever I had in my life' (*Diary*, 8 October 1662).

James took his duties seriously, chairing the weekly meetings of the newly constituted Board and drawing up regulations for the fleet, including one which optimistically docked a day's pay from any sailor heard cursing or swearing, and another ordering up to twelve lashes for anyone 'who pisseth on the decks'.[3] Pepys, who began by being somewhat in awe of him ('till now [I] did ever fear to meet him' – 4 March 1664), soon came to admire his powers of organisation, and was in turn obviously held high in the duke's estimation, to the point at which James was even prepared to take advice from the Clerk of the Acts. On 24 July 1668 Pepys recorded a momentous meeting with his chief:

After the Duke of York was ready, he called me to his closet, and there I did long and largely show him the weakness of our office, and did give him advice … which he did take mighty well, and desired me to draw up what I would have him write to the office. I did lay open the whole failings of the office, and how it was his duty to find them and to find fault with them, as Admiral … which he agreed to – and seemed much to rely on what I said.

However, administrative matters, while important, were not enough to satisfy the soldierly instincts of the Lord High Admiral, and it was not long before James sought an opportunity to prove himself as a leader in naval as well as in land warfare. At that time little distinction was made between the conduct of battles on land or sea, or indeed those who directed them. The title of General-at-Sea was given to naval officers better known for their military prowess on land, such as Charles II's nephew Prince Rupert or the Duke of Albemarle (the newly-ennobled General Monck).

THE WRITTEN WORD

Nowadays the names of the great Elizabethan writers are widely known, and their work is still generally appreciated, read and performed. Shakespeare, Marlowe, Spenser and their contemporaries need no introduction to today's students, readers and theatre audiences. Identifying the literary figures of the later seventeenth century might seem at first sight less easy, but in fact three of them, though equally well known, tend to be passed over because they were not writing in the usual fields of drama or poetry. Two were diarists and another penned a powerful religious work whilst in a prison cell. They were Samuel Pepys, John Evelyn and John Bunyan.

Some critics would argue that a diary cannot really qualify as literature. Pepys proves them wrong. For narrative flow, a cast of larger-than-life characters, keen observation of human nature, a wide range of emotions and a solid historical background, he has provided us with a work of genius, worthy to stand on a par with all the other great novels. Except, of course, that it is all true. Pepys left an invaluable record of his daily life and work in London covering the years 1660 until 1669, when he discontinued his famous *Diary* due to problems with his eyesight. Sadly, we therefore have no first-hand account from him of the events of 1688–89. Such a record would have been immensely valuable, especially in view of the fact that he himself was implicated in the Popish Plot. However, we do have many entries about James, Duke of York, which paint a word-picture of the duke in his days as Lord High Admiral – concerned for the Navy, conscientious and active, proud but approachable. He clearly held Pepys in high esteem, as indeed did his brother the king. It is astonishing that neither of them saw fit to give Pepys a knighthood.

Pepys came of comparatively humble stock (his father was a tailor), but it was family connections which eventually secured for him, as a young man, the appointment to the Navy Board which he was to fill with such distinction. The situation with John Evelyn was quite different. His father was a wealthy landowner and John, his second son, had no need to work. After Oxford and a period of European travel he settled down on his Deptford estate, Sayes Court, where he and his wife Mary brought up their children. Evelyn's life of faithful domesticity contrasts strongly with

Pepys' rather rackety existence, which was punctuated on an almost daily basis by amorous adventures of varying intensity. Yet despite their contrasting characters they became firm friends; Evelyn, wrote Pepys, was 'a very ingenious man and the more I know him, the more I love him' (29 April 1666).

Like Pepys, Evelyn moved in Government circles and filled various official posts; unlike Pepys, he was able to record the events of the Revolution at first hand and so to reinforce our more detailed knowledge of them. His own *Diary* flows along in an easy, informative style, though he is much less concerned with the *minutiae* of daily life than Pepys and comes across as a more austere observer. In fact he cultivated a detached attitude which enabled him to accept the post of Commissioner of the Privy Council from King James whilst sympathising with the cause of William and Mary and supporting their eventual arrival, something which Pepys could never have brought himself to do.

While Pepys and Evelyn were caught up in the daily affairs of this life, John Bunyan was more interested in the next one. The son of a tinker, whose trade he himself originally followed, he received only an elementary education, but nevertheless was able to develop a powerful, Biblically-inspired style of writing. Holding strong Protestant beliefs, he became an Independent preacher, for which he was twice imprisoned in Bedford gaol. During the first period, which lasted from 1660 until 1672 (but was not especially rigorous), he wrote nine books on religious themes including the opening chapters of his masterpiece *The Pilgrim's Progress*. During the second period, lasting for six months in 1676, he completed the work; it was published in 1678, and reappeared with a second part in 1684.

Although the narrative of Christian's journey through life may today have lost some of its moral impact, Bunyan's stately prose has become a treasured part of the national literary heritage. We can all recognise Vanity Fair, Doubting Castle, the Slough of Despond, as features in the landscapes of our own lives. Most of us have met Giant Despair at some point, and many may hope that their end will be like that of Mr Valiant-for-Truth: 'So he passed over, and all the trumpets sounded for him on the other side.'

Bunyan's work, despite its strong poetic element, is nevertheless prose. For the finest poetry of the age we turn to John Dryden, poet-laureate (1670), satirist and dramatist. Though he was not entirely without means, the need to make a living meant that he spent much of the first part of his career writing for the theatre, mostly heroic plays and comedies. His first great poem was *Absalom and Achitophel* (1681), a satirical commentary on the Popish Plot, but it did not appear until he was 50. The well-known *A Song for St. Cecilia's Day* (1687) was set to music by the Italian Giovanni Battista Draghi, long resident in London. A greater composer than Draghi was commemorated by Dryden in 1696 with *An Ode on the Death of Mr. Henry Purcell*, which was set by John Blow. The poem *Alexander's Feast* (1697) would later be given a musical setting by Handel, as would *A Song for St. Cecilia's Day* (Handel changed *Song* to *An Ode*).

After the accession of James II, Dryden converted to Catholicism; he refused to swear the oath of allegiance to William and Mary and so was deprived of his Laureateship and the pension which went with it. He made up the shortfall in his income by returning to playwriting and by translating the works of the Classical poets such as Virgil and Homer. He was a hugely prolific writer (he has been called 'the founder of modern English literary criticism'), and while his measured verse and topical political satire may not be to modern taste, there is no denying the enduring quality of his work or his stature as the leading literary figure of the late seventeenth century.

The Anglo-Dutch Wars of the seventeenth century were not primarily about politics, religion, or territory. They were about trade. Ever since the early 1600s, and even before, England had rightly perceived a threat to her commercial interests posed by the Dutch. This took the form of an aggressive Dutch policy supported by naval power on the high seas, most notably on the coast of West Africa, in the East Indies, and in the fledgling colonies of the New World. In addition the Dutch resented English claims to the right to control what were then called the Narrow Seas, i.e. the English Channel and the Irish Sea. English merchant ships were harassed, English merchants in their onshore settlements obstructed – sometimes violently – by the Dutch. The great spice-laden vessels of the London-based East India Company (founded in 1601) faced stiff competition from their opposite numbers of the Dutch East India Company based in Java. Meanwhile the English watched with mounting dismay and envy as the Dutch grew richer and their merchant fleets larger. 'The trade of the world is too little for us two, therefore one must down', later remarked the merchant seaman Captain George Cocke to his friend Samuel Pepys. What the Duke of York himself was later to call 'the several complaints of our Merchants of the injuries they received from the Dutch' could no longer be ignored.[4] It was clear that some action would have to be taken.

Failure on the part of a Dutch admiral to salute some English warships as they sailed past his squadron in the Channel afforded the pretext which triggered the First Anglo-Dutch War in 1652, during the Cromwellian Interregnum. The war lasted until 1654 and reached a decisive point at the Battle of Scheveningen in July 1653, at which the famous Admiral Tromp was killed and the Dutch heavily defeated. But this was a pyrrhic victory which solved nothing, and the old rivalries continued unabated, developing over the years into a sequence of tit-for-tat attacks on the trading fleets of both countries. Potent ingredients in this seething brew were the strongly protectionist if short-lived Navigation Acts of 1660 and 1663 which (updating an earlier Act of 1651) effectively closed English markets to foreign traders. The Acts also made things difficult by insisting that English goods had to be carried in English-built ships with mainly English crews.

To the Duke of York and his circle the situation amounted to unfinished business which could only be settled by preparing for all-out war. In the summer of 1664 James, aboard the warship *Swiftsure*, led the fleet for several days on exercises in the English Channel; this was in fact his first experience of actual command at sea. By the end of the event he had convinced himself that in any forthcoming war evidence of English naval superiority would force the Dutch to sue for peace.

And so the Second Anglo-Dutch War began in February 1665. The fleet that headed proudly out to sea a few weeks later, led by the duke on his flagship the *Royal Charles*, was the largest ever to have set sail from England. On 3 June it met up with the Dutch near Lowestoft and a fierce battle took place, ending with the rout of the Dutch fleet which lost seventeen ships in the engagement as against a single English vessel. The Duke of York displayed his usual cool courage in battle, although he was forcibly and unpleasantly reminded of his dangerous situation when a chain-shot ploughed through a group of three companions standing beside him. 'The Earl of Falmouth, [Lord] Muskery, and Mr R[ichard] Boyle [were] killed on board the Duke's ship the Royall Charles, with one shot. Their blood and brains flying in the Duke's face; and the head of Mr. Boyle striking down the Duke, as some say', wrote Pepys with gusto (8 June). This stark account is a reminder that naval battles of the seventeenth and eighteenth centuries, no less than those on land, were messy, brutal and bloody, far removed from the carefully choreographed events popularised by Hollywood in its vintage 'historical' epics.

It was perhaps this incident more than any other which temporarily alerted King Charles and his ministers to the folly of exposing the heir to the throne to such peril. Once the fleet had returned to port the Lord High Admiral was summoned back to London and command at sea was transferred to Pepys' patron the Earl of Sandwich. After a series of unfortunate misjudgements Sandwich was replaced by the Duke of Albemarle and Prince Rupert as joint commanders; their most memorable action was an inconclusive fight known as the Four Days' Battle, which took place in June 1666 off the North Foreland. Inconclusive it may have been, but the English nevertheless lost seventeen ships and some eight thousand men, the gunfire being clearly heard in the streets of London.

Life had not long returned to those same streets after the devastation of the Great Plague in the previous year. Against the background of the war a general nervousness now prevailed; this increased after the Four Days' Battle and was not helped by rumours, by the inevitable inaccurate reporting, or by the activities of the press gangs which – as later, in the eighteenth century – were empowered to seize fit men (many of them with families to support) when and where they could, to make up the crew numbers for the fleet. Pepys deplored the forcible abduction of these unwilling recruits 'that they have these two last nights pressed in the City out of houses – the persons wholly unfit for sea, and many of them people of very good fashion – which is a shame to think of … It is a great tyranny' (30 June, 1 July 1666). Nevertheless he reluctantly condoned the practice and made the necessary arrangements to ship the men (on this occasion numbering about 300) out to the fleet at sea.

It is safe to say that the Lord High Admiral did not share Pepys' concern for individuals; his interest was in the Navy at large, and he must have found the absence of firm information as frustrating as anybody else. When the news was good he was glad to pass it on: 'To St. James's … Here … before us all, the Duke of York did say that now at length he is come to a sure knowledge that the Dutch did lose in the late engagements 29 captains and 13 ships' (18 July). Other matters, which would have been contrary to his ideas of order and discipline, were no doubt kept from him. On 21 July Commissioner Peter Pett, in charge of Chatham naval dockyard, told Pepys 'how infinite the disorders are among the commanders and all officers of the fleet – no discipline – nothing but swearing and cursing, and everybody doing what they please'. This lax state of affairs was to some extent the fault of the duke himself, for many of the captains whom he had appointed were his personal friends, or had friends at court; they had no experience of the sea, or even of warfare, and in effect were answerable to nobody except the duke. As it happened, his own courage and powers of decisive leadership were about to be tested again in a unique and unexpected event.

On 2 September 1666, at about three o'clock in the morning, a small fire broke out on the premises of a baker in Pudding Lane, not far from St Paul's Cathedral. Fires were a constant hazard in most old cities at that time, but were usually brought under control before doing much more than localised damage. This one was different. Aided by the lethal combination of a strong wind and tinder-dry conditions after months of drought, it ignored all the puny efforts made to check it and began to race like a demon through the narrow alleyways and streets of the city (which were closely packed with timber-built houses), devouring everything in its path. Alerted by Samuel Pepys, whose vivid account of the Great Fire still ranks as one of the greatest-ever pieces of verbal on-the-spot reporting, King Charles and the Duke of York together soon realised that the city authorities, headed by a weak and ineffectual Lord Mayor, were quite unable to cope with the situation. The royal brothers surveyed the progress of the fire from their barge on the river, and gave orders for the wholesale blowing-up of large swathes of buildings to create fire-breaks. But the duke also imposed his personal authority on the ground, by riding around the threatened areas at the head of a detachment of soldiers, both to exercise crowd-control and also to give help to the distressed citizens. This was just the kind of emergency in which James excelled, and he worked actively at the head of his men to try to save buildings and to rescue victims – 'even labouring in person, & being present, to command, order, reward, and encourage Workemen', as Evelyn put it.[5] The crackling of flames, the crash of falling timbers, the cries of anguish – these, after all, were to him a familiar background of sound reminding him of the heat of battle and his role as a commander both on land and at sea.

Gradually the Great Fire died down, leaving many acres of smoking, ruined buildings – a sad jumble of homes, shops, livery halls, churches, even the great Gothic cathedral of St Paul itself – and many more wrecked lives. Against the background of this devastation the war dragged on, with advantage to neither side. However, things took a far more serious turn in June 1667 with the sudden, unexpected and most unwelcome appearance of the Dutch fleet in the Medway. The invaders sailed up the river with impunity, took Sheerness, broke through a huge defensive iron chain which stretched from bank to bank, and arrived at Chatham where they burnt eight men-of-war before sailing back out to sea unchallenged. Most humiliating of all, they boarded the unguarded *Royal Charles* and towed it away, changing its name (again) and converting it to their own use. This action effectively ended the war and on the following 31 July at Breda a peace treaty was signed in which, in a cynical *volte-face*, the English and Dutch now agreed to join forces against the French. A minor but more enduring clause ensured that the Dutch colony and city of New Amsterdam in America, which had already been taken by an expeditionary force sent out by James in 1664, was now officially ceded to England and was renamed New York in honour of the duke. Otherwise the English got little from the treaty except humiliation. They were compelled to give up claims to territory including Surinam in South America (which then became Dutch Guiana) and the spice island of Run in the Malay Archipelago. Restrictions formerly imposed on Dutch trading practices were lifted, and the area of open sea in which the English demanded a salute as of right was greatly reduced.[6]

The Treaty of Breda brought a breathing space, but not peace. While smarting under the terms of the treaty, England had not forgotten the insult of the Medway incident, and still seethed with resentment. More importantly, both Charles II and Louis XIV were in agreement that the Dutch had got above themselves and needed to be taught a lesson. Secret negotiations took place with the French, who were easily weaned off the alliance which they had formerly had with the Dutch, and agreed to supplement the proposed English fleet of fifty warships with another thirty of their own. Other, potentially explosive issues were also raised in the negotiations, as will be seen. On 17 March 1672 war was declared on the Netherlands for the third time in twenty years, and the Lord High Admiral once again found himself at the centre of events, for the king – putting aside his earlier qualms – had agreed that James was again to be in command of the fleet at sea, with Lord Sandwich as deputy. One month later in April the Admiral set sail from the Nore off Sheerness on his flagship *Prince*, a newly built 'first-rater' of 100 guns, and began to search for the Dutch fleet under its commander, the celebrated Admiral de Ruyter.

After some preliminary manoeuvres the two fleets finally met up in Southwold Bay (then known as Solebay) on 28 May and the calm sea soon became turbulent with all the violence of a seventeenth-century naval battle. Things became so hot that James was forced to move from the *Prince* to the *St Michael* and then later to the *London*; before the final transfer could be made he was kept bobbing about in a rowing boat for almost an hour in the thick of the conflict.[7] Only one English warship, the *Royal James*, was actually lost, and with it went down the Earl of Sandwich. When after several days his charred body was washed ashore – one of many hundreds which were buried in churchyards all along the coastline – the only identification was the Garter star sewn onto his coat and three rings in a pocket.[8]

Some idea of the carnage involved in these naval battles can be gleaned by studying the paintings and drawings of the celebrated marine artists Willem van de Velde and his son, of the same name and sometimes considered to be greater than his father. As the seventeenth-century equivalent of today's photo-journalist, the elder Willem was present on the Dutch side at the battles of Scheveving, Lowestoft, the Four Days' Battle, and Solebay. He then switched sides and moved in 1672 to England, where he and his son were made much of by Charles II, who commissioned works from them and gave them every facility to pursue their art. So great was the king's respect for the elder Willem that he banned the eager artist, who was already over 60 years old, from being present at the Battle of Texel (one of the West Frisian islands), which took place on 21 August 1673 (NS) and was the final naval battle of the Third Anglo-Dutch War.[9] Instead the event was recorded by the younger Willem in a large oil painting which is said to be one of his finest works; it is now in the National Maritime Museum at Greenwich. In a drawing of the Battle of Scheveningen (also in the Museum), the elder Willem depicted himself sitting in a small sailing boat on the fringes of the battle, sketching the action as it unfolded before him. It has been suggested that a pen-and-ink plan of a yacht by the younger Willem (in the Dutch Maritime Museum) might be of a boat specifi- cally intended to take himself and his father out to record the battle scenes.[10] Determination and bravery, as well as natural artistic talent, were clearly two of the essential elements in the highly personal style of both the elder and younger van de Velde.

After Texel no further important actions took place; the war gradually petered out and was finally brought to an ignominious end which was hastened by the refusal of Parliament to grant the king any more money for supplies. The concluding peace treaty was signed at Westminster on 28 February 1674. By that time the Lord High Admiral had already resigned his post, and had been succeeded in his command at sea by his uncle Prince Rupert. His naval career had come to an end. But it was not incompetence, adverse criticism or lack of self-confidence that caused his resignation – it was religion.

It is impossible to say when exactly James decided to become a professed Roman Catholic. It might be thought that he had been persuaded to do so by his mother, during the years of exile in France, but it seems that at that time he not only resisted her arguments but also took her to task for trying to exert the same kind of pressure on his brother Charles. More probably it was pressure from a different source that caused him to search his conscience and to begin to tread the path that led eventually to full conversion. In 1660 he married Anne Hyde, daughter of Edward Hyde, at the time Charles II's Lord Chancellor and a powerful minister. She became a secret convert to Catholicism, probably soon after their marriage (although her husband put her conversion at around 1670), and so may well have had considerable influence on James in religious matters.[11] She even wrote an essay, mainly for his benefit, in which she explained the reasons behind her conversion, chief amongst these being that the origins of the Church of England were based not on sound doctrine but on purely personal and political grounds, especially the scandal of Henry VIII's divorce.[12]

It might sometimes seem that James' private life was staid and that he himself did not share his brother's notorious sexual appetites. Nothing could be further from the truth. Although little is known about his earlier escapades, after marriage he entertained a long sequence of mistresses, and in fact his union with Anne began with her (or his) seduction in the mid-1650s at the court of his exiled brother, where she was a Maid of Honour to the Princess Mary.[13] In November 1659 there was even a marriage of sorts, after which Anne became pregnant. Led on by his mother, his sister and others to believe that he was not the father, James at first tried to wriggle out of the involvement, but the king would not hear of it. He sympathised with Chancellor Hyde, who had been deeply upset by these developments, locking his daughter in her room and threatening to throw her out of the house. There would now be a proper wedding, pronounced Charles grimly, meanwhile elevating Hyde to the barony of Clarendon. It was a quiet event, held privately on 3 September 1660 in the Clarendons' London mansion on fashionable Piccadilly. Little more than a month later the Yorks' firstborn appeared (a son, named Charles) but did not live. Over time a sad little procession of eight babies was to follow, only two of whom – both girls – would survive to adulthood. They were the future queens Mary and Anne.

Gossip swirled around the affair, mostly uninformed. On 7 October Samuel Pepys' employer and patron, Lord Sandwich, told him 'that the Duke of Yorke hath got my Lord Chancellor's daughter with child … And that the King would have him to marry her, but that he will not.' In fact it was then already over a month since the wedding had taken place. In a pungent and picturesque comment on the situation, 'my Lord told me that among his father's many old sayings … this is one: that he that doth get a wench with child and marries her afterward it is as if a man should shit in his hat and then clap it upon his head.' Throughout this conversation Lord Sandwich spoke in French, so that the servants should not understand – a classic case of *pas devant les domestiques*.

Anne was not famed for her good looks. Pepys – surely something of a connoisseur in such matters – described her bluntly and perhaps unkindly as 'a plain woman, and like her mother, my Lady Chanceller' (20 April 1661). At the other end of the spectrum her portrait by Peter Lely shows a good-looking woman, certainly not plain. But inevitably Lely saw her through the rose-tinted spectacles of the court painter, and in fact – as is so often the case – the truth probably lay somewhere in between. Whatever she may have lacked in looks, she made up for in strength of character, especially boldness and determination, and this led to accusations of pride.[14]

A feature of the gossip surrounding the Duke of York and reported to Pepys was that the duchess 'is very troublesome to him by [reason of] her jealousy' (15 May 1663). She had good cause. The duke made no secret of his various amours: 'Nay, he hath come out of his wife's bed, and gone to others laid in bed for him' (24 June 1667). Even so she was prepared to put up with his escapades for the sake of her position and authority, and indeed not only her own. Because of her status, her father Lord Clarendon could not be called to account for mismanagement of the nation's affairs – notably the shameful 1667 peace treaty of Breda, for which he was somewhat unfairly blamed – and this caused some public unrest. Anne died in 1671, 'very little beloved and not much lamented',[15] and in her final days begged her husband to stay at her bedside, ensuring that no Anglican clergy were allowed near her, so that she could receive the last rites of her own Church unhindered by their unwelcome attentions.[16]

James' Catholic sympathies were already public knowledge as early as 1661. On 18 February that year Samuel Pepys, having heard a wild rumour that the king was already secretly married and had two sons, declared himself 'gladder that it should be so, than that the Duke of York and his family should come to the Crown – he being a professed friend to the Catholiques'. It is probable that James had become a committed Catholic by the late 1660s, in belief if not in practice. He himself confidently pinned down his conversion to a definite date: 'In the beginning of the year 1669 ... His R[oyal] H[ighness] was more sensibly touched in conscience, and began to think seriously of his Salvation.'[17]

He now accepted without question the complete supremacy of the Church of Rome and its teachings and consequently, like his wife, totally rejected the validity of Anglican Orders.[18] In 1669, aware that his brother the king secretly shared many of his beliefs, he had tried to persuade Charles to use the promise of his – Charles' – full and open conversion to Catholicism as a bargaining counter in a new approach to Louis XIV. Contact was made and, being well received by Louis, resulted in the secret treaty which had enabled Charles to renew hostilities with the Dutch in 1672. The treaty provided that, in return for both financial and military support, Charles would publicly declare himself a Catholic.[19] It was actually signed in Dover Castle in May 1670 by Charles and James, and – on behalf of Louis – by their youngest sister Henriette, who had come over from France expressly for the purpose, although the pretext for her visit was the king's 40th birthday. Her status was that of Louis' sister-in-law, since she was married to his brother Philip, Duke of Orleans, known at the French court as 'Monsieur, the King's brother', or indeed simply as 'Monsieur'. Sadly, she died only three weeks later.

When it came to the point, Charles foresaw all too clearly the strife and bloodshed that would result from any attempt to impose Catholicism at home. He was far too canny to go along with the idea, and in February 1672 the treaty (or 'the Grand Design', as it was known) was finally though not publicly revealed, in truncated form and without any reference to religious change. War against the Dutch was declared on the following 17 March, as has been seen. Two days earlier Charles had gone as far as he dared, by issuing a Declaration of Indulgence which released Non-conformists and – significantly – Catholics from the legal penalties which since 1593 (in the case of Catholics) had prevented them from openly practising their religions. The Declaration was partly a genuine attempt to correct what Charles had long considered an injustice, but it was also a reflection of some of the pressure which he himself felt as a probable closet Catholic. Nevertheless it was destined to fail.

It failed because it came up against the implacable and immovable obstacle of Parliament. In 1662 Charles had tried without success to get Parliament to ratify a similar agreement. Now, ten years later, he completely ignored Parliament, which had not met since April 1671, and presented the Declaration as a *fait accompli*. All might have been well, if there had not been a need to raise money to continue the war with the Dutch – which meant that Parliament had to be recalled. Summoned back to Westminster in February 1673, the MPs were in a bad mood, specifically over the Declaration. The king, they asserted, had overstepped the mark and had no authority whatever to exercise supreme power in ecclesiastical matters. They resented what they perceived as his high-handed dealings and moreover, only too aware of his brother's by now well-known Catholic sympathies, suspected that the Declaration was merely a device to make things easier all round for Catholics in general. So furious was the opposition that Charles was forced to withdraw it, in return for a provisional grant of £70,000 per month over an eighteen-month period. [20] However, the king's humiliating climb-down was not enough to satisfy the Members, who after many months' inactivity were keen to re-assert their importance, and they decided to introduce a measure of their own. This was the Test Act.

The Test Act of 1673 was the very antithesis of the Declaration. As its title indicated, it tested the suitability of those holding or seeking public office, who were now required to reject by oath the Catholic doctrine of transubstantiation (i.e. the belief that the bread and wine taken at Holy Communion are changed into the actual body and blood of Christ). The Act also required office-holders to receive the Sacrament according to the rites of the Church of England. The Act contained other provisions, but these two were the main ones, and they ensured the exclusion of Catholics from any meaningful official post for the foreseeable future. Originally the Act was not applied to peers, but in 1678 it was extended to include them. In any case its message was clear enough, and it finally made James' position as Lord High Admiral untenable.

At Easter 1672, in a bold act of defiance or a strong statement of personal belief (depending on how one looks at it), he had failed to join the king in publicly taking Communion according to the Anglican rite. The following year, 'to the amazement of everybody' he made the same stand. There could no longer be any doubts about his beliefs and intentions, which, wrote John Evelyn, 'gave exceeding griefe & scandal to the whole Nation … What the Consequence of this will be God onely knows, & Wise men dread' (30 March 1673).

Sadly, yet more grief and scandal were to follow. In the autumn of 1673, only a few months after the introduction of the Test Act and having already resigned his office as Lord High Admiral, James married again. In the circumstances the choice of bride – an Italian Catholic – could hardly have been more unfortunate. Sent to scour the European courts for a suitable candidate, King Charles' emissary the Earl of Peterborough came up with a winner – Maria Beatrice Isabella d'Este, daughter of the Duke of Modena. She was tall, dark-haired and good-looking, and had been well educated. It mattered not that she had been 'so innocently bred' that she had never before heard of England, let alone the Duke of York, and had designs to become a nun.[21] James was enthusiastic, and a proxy marriage ceremony was held on 20 September (30 September NS), with Lord Peterborough standing in for the groom.[22] A few days later, on 25 September (her birthday), she set sail for England, chaperoned by her mother and stopping in Paris en route to visit Louis XIV. They arrived at Dover on 23 November and were welcomed by James, who was so keen to proceed with the marriage that a second ceremony was held that same day. The bride was just 15 years old, her husband 35. It cannot have done much for his self-confidence that, in the early days of the marriage, his wife burst into tears every time she set eyes on him.

News of the impending marriage had leaked out even before the new Duchess of York (whose name would henceforth be anglicised as Mary) had left France. In October Parliament petitioned the king that James' marriage should not be recognised. The MPs were told (untruthfully) that since the marriage had already taken place nothing could be done, and as a means of avoiding further trouble the king then suspended Parliament, which did not meet again until the following January. On 5 November Evelyn wrote in his *Diary*: 'This night the youths of the Citty burnt the Pope in Effigie after they had made procession with it in great triumph; displeased at the D[uke] for altering his Religion, & now marrying an Italian lady &c.' The omens for political and social harmony were not good.

PLOTS AND POPERY

*J*ames' resignation as Lord High Admiral and his very public withdrawal from Anglican church services signalled his Catholicism as plainly as any message he had ever ordered to be flagged from ship to ship. However, not only did it otherwise make no difference to his involvement in the daily affairs of Government, but it also embroiled him in destructive arguments with powerful figures such as Lord Shaftesbury.

Astute, able, self-serving and devious, Anthony Ashley-Cooper (as he then was) had been at one time a supporter of Cromwell, but had switched sides and worked for the restoration of the monarchy. For this service he was duly rewarded, becoming Baron Ashley and Chancellor of the Exchequer in 1661. Samuel Pepys formed a good if superficial impression of him: 'I find my Lord … a very ready, quick and diligent person' (27 May 1663). After the fall of Clarendon in 1667, Ashley threw in his lot with four other noblemen; the five together then formed an unofficial but powerful inner cabinet of advisors around the king. They were known collectively as the Cabal, a portmanteau word derived from the initial letters of their names, which were lords Clifford and Arlington, the Duke of Buckingham, Ashley himself, and the Duke of Lauderdale. (Apparently it was a coincidence – though certainly a strangely convenient one – that the same word was and still is used to indicate any group or clique of political schemers.) In 1672 Ashley was elevated to the Earldom of Shaftesbury and named Lord Chancellor, although he was not to hold the post for long.

As a means of deflecting public criticism over the conduct of the war, the newly ennobled Lord Shaftesbury took up the Protestant cause with apparent enthusiasm, supporting the Test Act and criticising the Duke of York's marriage to Mary of Modena. He had never been a favourite with the duke, who now took a positive dislike to him and urged King Charles to demand the return of the Great Seal (the Lord Chancellor's symbol of office). The king – no longer as impressed by Shaftesbury as he had once been – complied; in November 1673 the earl was forced to resign, and the Cabal fell apart. Its place as the king's chief body of advisors was taken by James himself, together with the former Sir Thomas Osborne, now created Earl of Danby, an able administrator who from 1667 to 1673 had been Treasurer of the Navy and for whom James had some admiration – which, however, was not to last.

James' growing disenchantment with Lord Danby had two main causes, of which the first was again based on religious differences. Danby was a staunch Anglican, and while it seems that James had originally hoped to convert him to Catholicism, those hopes were soon dashed.[1] In fact Danby went out of his way to try to ensure that Catholics and Non-conformists alike were barred from any kind of public service, and that existing laws on this theme were strictly enforced. By various means (not excluding bribery), he also tried to build up strong pro-Royalist, Anglican-based support within the House of Commons. A Bill which he brought before Parliament and which would have further reinforced the restrictions of the Test Act failed only because of a row over procedure which blew up between the Lords and Commons.

The second cause of James' discontent was the conduct of foreign affairs. Danby had expected that a more pro-Royalist Parliament would be better inclined to vote for the necessary funds to prop up the king's shaky finances. Instead, the MPs made this conditional on the king's showing some readiness to sever ties with the unpopular French and to realign England on the side of the Dutch, joining forces with them in military opposition to Louis XIV – for Louis had not been party to the 1674 Treaty of Westminster and his troops were still waging war on Dutch soil. For months King Charles prevaricated, resisting both Parliamentary and public pressure to split up from Louis (from whom he continued to receive secret subsidies), and several times proroguing and then recalling a rebellious Parliament. There were those who thought that the stalemate could be resolved only by dissolution, pointing out that Parliament had already been sitting, on and off, for fifteen years. Meanwhile the growing threat of a gulf between England and France worried the Duke of York, whose sympathies were naturally with the French and whose current thinking envisaged not only the dissolution of Parliament but its sequel of an absolute monarchy supported and funded by King Louis.[2] The extent to which he was swimming against the tide was soon to be revealed, and it was much nearer to home than he would have wished.

Although both sides had claimed victory in the 1672 Battle of Solebay, it actually ended in stalemate. On the other hand, the Dutch forces on land seemed to be facing certain defeat as the invading army of Louis XIV quickly overran the provinces of Utrecht and Gelderland. However, it was at this point in the campaign that the invaders, and indeed Louis himself, received a nasty shock. Using their man-made terrain as a defensive weapon, the Dutch breached their own dykes, opened their sluices, and flooded the landscape, creating an ever-widening morass that gradually brought the French to a soggy halt. While the action itself was sanctioned by the States-General of the Netherlands, the military strategy behind this bold act of defiance was supplied by Prince William of Orange.

William's parents were the elder William of Orange and Mary, the eldest sister of Charles II and the Duke of York. The younger William was born on 14 November 1650 (NS), already orphaned by the death of his father only eight days previously. He received a strict Protestant upbringing at the hands of various learned tutors, and from 1659 until 1666 studied at the University of Leiden. His mother, who despite her position disliked the Netherlands and had taken little interest in his upbringing, died from smallpox on 24 December 1660 at Whitehall Palace whilst visiting her brothers.

As William grew up, strong republican elements headed by the powerful Dutch politician Johan de Witt tried to prevent his appointment as Stadtholder or chief magistrate, fearing that this would give too much power to the House of Orange. However, with the threat of war followed by its onset in March 1672 and the subsequent French invasion, William's undoubted abilities as a soldier – despite his youth and inexperience – could no longer be ignored. In February the States-General appointed him Captain-General of the army, and on 4 July he was confirmed in office as Stadtholder.[3]

Back in 1670, at a time when he was beginning to play a visible part in politics, William had been allowed by de Witt to pay a visit to his uncle Charles in England, to try and get the king to repay a large debt (over 2 million guilders) owed to the House of Orange. Needless to say – given the parlous state of the royal finances – he failed. In addition, he greatly disliked what he saw of his two uncles' dissolute life-style, which contrasted strongly with the moralistic atmosphere of his own. For his part Charles, who had been prepared to see his nephew in a favourable light, was put off by William's Calvinistic leanings, and also seems to have thought that William's strong patriotism could be a barrier in reaching a future political understanding with the Dutch.[4]

In July 1674 Lord Arlington arrived in the Netherlands, sent by King Charles to sound out the possibilities of persuading William to make peace. At the time these negotiations came to nothing, but it may well have been on the same occasion that an interesting suggestion was made. This was that marriage between William and the Duke of York's eldest surviving daughter Mary could be advantageous to both sides. Needless to say the duke himself was not pleased. Although the king had not allowed him to bring up his daughters as Catholics, James was certainly opposed to the idea of Mary marrying so doughty a Protestant champion as William of Orange. But the proposition had intrigued William, and he took steps to find out as much about the Princess Mary as he could. An important source of information was Sir William Temple, English Ambassador to The Hague and an enthusiast for good Anglo-Dutch relations. However, even more useful in this respect was Sir William's wife, one of whose closest friends was Mary's governess.[5] Persuaded by their favourable reports, William made up his mind.

By the summer of 1677 King Charles was under considerable pressure, both in the House of Commons and in the country at large, to help the Dutch in forcing the French out of Dutch territory. Then in the autumn William arrived in person, willing to discuss terms – but not until he had received permission to marry Mary. The Duke of York tried to put off the all-important decision, but was overruled by his brother, who insisted that the marriage must go ahead – which it did, at Whitehall on 4 November, the Bishop of London (Henry Compton) officiating. The date was also William's birthday. By all accounts the wedding was a sombre affair, although King Charles did his best to cheer everyone up, including making some rather off-colour jokes and encouraging the groom with such phrases as 'Hey, nephew, to your work! St. George for England!' [6] The guests could hardly fail to notice the marked physical contrast between bride and groom – she, a tall, lively and attractive dark-haired girl of 15; he, a short, round-shouldered, hook-nosed asthmatic of 26 whose appearance strongly belied his reputation as a military hero. William, in fact, was the very antithesis of the kind of man a dreamy teenager might have hoped to marry, whether in the seventeenth or twenty-first centuries.

The guests might also have been intrigued by similarities between Mary and her Italian stepmother. The two princesses shared the same first name, were of a similar age (Mary of Modena was the elder by four years), looked somewhat alike, and were both known to have shed copious tears on learning the identities of their prospective husbands. However, whatever the newly-weds themselves may have felt on that November day, news of the wedding was well received in the country at large; bonfires were lit, and countless glasses and pewter tankards were raised to the health of the happy pair. It has sometimes been suggested that Mary's early years of marriage were an unhappy time during which William bent his high-spirited young wife to his will with some severity. It is only fair to say that, after an unpromising start, William and Mary became in time a devoted and loving couple, and that William was devastated by Mary's untimely and much lamented death from smallpox at the age of 33 (1694).

PORTRAITS AND PANORAMAS

On 20 October 1662 Samuel Pepys visited a fashionable society painter to see if this artist would be willing to paint his portrait. He was told that it would be three weeks before anything could be done – 'which methinks is a rare thing'. Nor was this all. 'And then, to see in what pomp his table was laid for himself to go to dinner!' Pepys' belief that the artist had got ideas above his station was still as strong several years later: 'A mighty proud man he is, and full of state' (25 March 1667).

The 'mighty proud man' was Peter Lely. Pepys calls him Mr Lilly, and this seems to have been the generally accepted form of his name at the time. In fact his real name was Pieter van der Faes, born in 1618 of Dutch parents at Soest in Westphalia. He trained in Haarlem and arrived in London in the early 1640s. By 1650 he had a large studio specialising in portraits; he survived the rigours of the Commonwealth and in 1661 was appointed Principal Painter to Charles II. A constant flow of flattering portraits issued from the studio in his house on the fashionable Covent Garden piazza, amongst them the famous series of ten court Beauties (originally at Windsor but now at Hampton Court), which celebrates some of the women who captivated society at the time by their looks and/or sexual wiles. Even today they exert a strong sensual power as they gaze provocatively out at us with languorous, half-hooded eyes.

In these and in his portraits generally Lely shows his skill in capturing a likeness, as well as his technical virtuosity in conveying – with the help of studio assistants – not only the appearance but the actual texture of silks, satins and other drapery. His fashionable sitters did not want in-depth analysis of their personalities, they wanted good, flattering likenesses, and this is exactly what they got. Lely too got what he wanted, which was money and prestige, although the knighthood which he also coveted was not granted until the year of his death, 1680. James as Duke of York was painted several times by Lely, perhaps most notably in a double portrait with his first duchess, the former Anne Hyde, who is said to have commissioned the Hampton Court series herself. In 1677 Lely also painted the 15-year-old Princess Mary, at about the time of her marriage to William of Orange.

Lely's successor was already waiting in the wings. He was Gottfried Kniller of Lubeck (b. 1646), who had studied in Amsterdam under Rembrandt's pupil Ferdinand Bol, travelled in Europe as a portraitist, and arrived in London in 1674. A portrait of Charles II quickly won him fashionable recognition, and on Lely's death in 1680 he filled the royal position of Principal Painter, having long since changed his name to Godfrey Kneller. He was popular with sitters because he needed only an hour or so in which to capture a likeness – an ability which was his special gift – before completing the face himself (it helped that gentlemen wore large periwigs at the time) and then turning the work over to numerous studio/workshop assistants who would supply the details of hands, dress and background from established sources. In fact the whole process amounted to an artistic conveyor-belt, although it must be said that those of Kneller's portraits to which he gave extra personal attention show that he could produce rewarding work when he put his mind to it.

Kneller's reputation in no way suffered from his methods. On the contrary his natural arrogance and self-esteem received a further boost when he was asked by Queen Mary to paint another series of ten Beauties to rival that of Lely, on completion of which he received a knighthood in 1692. (This series is also at Hampton Court.) His opulent life-style far exceeded that of Lely; he travelled about in a coach-and-six and built himself a mansion near Twickenham which, as Kneller Hall, is now the home of the Royal Military School of Music. He died in 1723, having been created a baronet by King George I in 1715.

Such portraits by Lely and Kneller as are full-length and life-size are of necessity large, but they are dwarfed by the work of those artists who took walls and ceilings as their canvases and filled them with painted assemblies of classical heroes, monarchs, courtiers, soldiers and servants, presided over by cloud-borne gods and cherubs floating in bright blue skies or tumbling down the walls, all framed in splendid painted architectural settings like stage scenery. In fact there is an element of the theatrical in all these works, whose huge scale and flamboyant execution represented a style of decorative painting almost unknown in England until the early 1670s. It came from Italy, where it flourished as a branch of that florid, over-the-top art movement known as the Baroque, and was brought to these shores in or about 1672 by a Neapolitan painter, Antonio Verrio (b. *c.* 1639).

Verrio soon came to the attention of Charles II and was asked to decorate a royal suite of new rooms currently being constructed at Windsor Castle. This work occupied him, on and off, for the next twenty or so years, though most was destroyed during the reign of George IV. At the same time he worked on other commissions in great houses such as Burghley House, Ham House and Chatsworth.

On his accession in 1685 James II ordered the construction of a magnificent new Catholic chapel near the Banqueting House. (Sadly, it was destroyed by fire, together with most of the old palace of Whitehall, in 1698.) Great artists such as Wren and Grinling Gibbons were involved, and the decoration of walls and ceilings was entrusted to Verrio, who covered them with paintings celebrating the Blessed Virgin. As a Catholic himself he was not ready to welcome William and Mary, and withdrew for some years to live as the honoured guest of his patron the Earl of Exeter at Burghley, for whom he painted another great sequence of state rooms.

Like Lely and Keller, Verrio had a strong sense of his own importance, and his insistence on luxuries such as a constant supply of Parmesan cheese and his own coach and horses eventually began to pall. And so it was probably his employer Lord Exeter who in 1700 finally persuaded him to accept William's pressing invitation to work at Hampton Court. Here his most substantial contribution was to paint the walls of the King's Grand Staircase with a huge and complicated allegorical scene in which William himself appears as Alexander the Great. The work was finished in 1702, but the king probably had time to appreciate most of it before his death early in that year. Verrio himself died in 1707 but his style was continued by two other great decorative artists, the Frenchman Louis Laguerre (d. 1721) and the Englishman James Thornhill (d. 1734).

In February 1678, three months after the marriage, there appeared an inflammatory pamphlet entitled *An Account of the Growth of Popery and Arbitrary Government in England.* The author (though sensibly remaining anonymous) was Andrew Marvell, MP and former secretarial assistant to Cromwell, but better known today as a fine lyric poet. In the pamphlet Marvell warned his readers that there was a plot afoot 'to change the lawful Government of England into an absolute Tyranny and to convert the established Protestant religion into downright Popery'.[7] While Marvell's *Account* was by no means an isolated example, the pamphlet reflected the general sense of unease that England's Protestant heritage – so hard won – was under threat, both from creeping Catholicism at home and from aggressive French policies abroad. Some kind of concentrated public reaction was bound to come, and so it did, in the form of the infamous 'Popish Plot'.

The Plot had in fact been concocted by Titus Oates, an unsavoury Anglican cleric who in 1678 was aged 29. While the known facts of his earlier life are somewhat confused, they nevertheless present a portrait of a consummate rogue. After having been received into the Catholic Church in 1677, he had spent some time training unsuccessfully to be a Jesuit priest in seminaries at Valladolid in Spain and St Omer in France, from both of which he was ejected. This was not a new experience for him, as he had already been expelled from Merchant Taylors' school and from two Cambridge colleges (St John's and Gonville and Caius) which he left without securing a degree, and had been drummed out of, first, his Anglican parish in Kent and then, a naval chaplaincy on HMS *Adventurer.* His ejection from his parish followed a trumped-up accusation of sodomy – at that time a capital offence – which for some reason he had made against a young schoolmaster. The case was dismissed and Oates instead received a heavy fine and a spell of imprisonment in Dover Castle. The situation was reversed when he got his marching orders from the *Adventurer* after being accused of a serious crime, none other than – surprise! – sodomy. Only his Anglican orders saved him from the gallows.[8]

His flirtation with Catholicism had undoubtedly been opportunist rather than prompted by genuine conviction, and indeed he later asserted that his patriotic aim all along had been to penetrate the Jesuit organisation and to uncover its secret plans. No doubt he also wanted to replace the contempt and derision, in which so far he had been generally held, with a measure of fame and public recognition. Even Nature had been unkind to him, giving him bow legs, a strangely pig-like face attached to a bull neck, and a harsh, strident voice. The time was now ripe for him to take his revenge.

Egged on by his friend Israel Tonge, another fanatical and unbalanced Anglican priest, Oates now produced a long list of accusations against English Catholics in general and the Jesuits in particular. The gist of this was that there existed a plot to assassinate Charles II and to replace him with James, with military help from France. As a result, England would become a Catholic country once again. Oates stopped short of implicating James himself; instead he presented the Duke of York as an innocent catspaw who would himself be destroyed if he refused to go along with the plotters. Already – alleged Oates – there had been a meeting of leading Jesuits, at which final plans had been discussed. Although recently there had indeed been such a meeting (though not to promote rebellion), Oates was fortunately unaware that it had been held at Whitehall on the duke's own premises, otherwise things could have gone badly wrong for James.

Summoned to appear before the Privy Council on 28 September 1678 to explain his accusations, Oates made the most of his opportunity. It seems that, despite all his other disadvantages, he was quite an impressive orator; Chief Justice Francis North 'once heard Oates preach at St. Dunstan's, and much admired his theatrical behaviour in the pulpit'.[9] On this occasion his performance failed to convince King Charles, but others were not so sure. Oates left the council chamber with authority to order the immediate arrest of minor figures on his list of suspects – which included many Jesuits as well as noblemen from the old Catholic families – and went to work with gusto.

He had already been instructed – probably by Lord Danby, who was prepared to give him some credibility – to swear an affidavit as to the truth of his accusations. This he did on 6 September before a popular justice of the peace (JP), Sir Edmund Berry Godfrey. A little over a month later Sir Edmund's body was discovered on Primrose Hill, transfixed by his own sword. Although the circumstances surrounding his death were far from clear (some, including the king and the Duke of York, believed it to have been suicide), the coroner's jury nevertheless returned a verdict of murder. This was a gift to Titus Oates, who promptly and publicly identified the 'Papists', especially the Jesuits, as the killers, and launched a propaganda campaign warning of an imminent pogrom of Protestants which, had it ever taken place, would have been on the scale of the 1572 St Bartholomew's Day Massacre in Paris. The public response was immediate and violent; those suspected, rightly or wrongly, of being Catholics found all too soon that 'nothing could resist the fury of the people that, like a hurricane, pursued them'.[10] Inflamed by a constant stream of rumours, scurrilous pamphlets and broadsheets, riots broke out, anti-Catholic mobs roamed the streets, effigies of the Pope were publicly burned, premises were searched for arms, and for their own protection society ladies armed themselves with daggers inscribed *Remember Justice Godfrey*.[11] The widespread arrests of alleged plotters and their sympathisers were followed by trials presided over by the blatantly partisan Chief Justice, Sir William Scroggs. Over thirty executions followed, many of the victims (mostly priests) being convicted on the fraudulent testimony of Oates himself.

It is sometimes supposed that the more barbaric forms of execution – in particular, hanging, drawing and quartering, and even burning at the stake – were a speciality of the medieval and Tudor periods and would not have been still in use by the late seventeenth century. Sadly, this was not so, and these horrific public events continued to attract large crowds of sightseers. Even Samuel Pepys could not keep away; on 13 October 1660 he 'went out to Charing Cross to see Maj.-Gen. Harrison hanged, drawn, and quartered – which was done there – he looking as cheerfully as any man could do in that condition. He was presently cut down, and his head and his heart shown to the people, at which there was great shouts of joy.' Harrison was one of eleven regicides executed in the same gruesome manner over a period of a fortnight.

Oates' allegations were given some credibility by the discovery of some very indiscreet letters written to Jesuit contacts in France by Edward Coleman, a Catholic convert who had been secretary to the Duke of York and was now attached to the household of Mary of Modena in the same capacity. The letters dealt generally though not specifically with the highly topical themes of setting up links with France and re-establishing Catholicism in England. Although they were written in a private capacity their effect was no less powerful than if they had been written by the duke himself, and they appeared to reinforce strongly the allegations of Oates and his associates. Coleman was tried in November and duly executed on 3 December. Ironically, it was the exposure of Coleman's intrigues that was Oates' only genuine contribution to the anti-Catholic movement. His status was now absurdly high with Parliament (recalled from another prorogation on 21 October), as well as with the public in general, and in the words of John Evelyn, 'the Commons ... had so exalted him, that they tooke for Gospell all he said, & without more ado, ruin'd all whom he nam'd to be Conspirators, nor did he spare whomsoever came in his way' (18 July 1679). Evelyn also found him to be, at different times, 'a bold man, & ... furiously indiscreet ... A vaine, insolent man'. When Oates, without a shred of evidence, accused five elderly Catholic peers of plotting to assassinate the king, the MPs had no hesitation in ordering their arrest and committal to the Tower.

As is often the case with would-be tyrants and despots, Oates now overreached himself. In an interview with King Charles on 24 November 1678, he boldly denounced the queen who, he said, was scheming with the royal physician, Sir George Wakeman, to poison her husband. In his later years Charles had grown much closer to the dignified and outwardly self-possessed Catherine, as indeed she had to him, and the word-picture of her painted by Oates, as some kind of contemporary Lucrezia Borgia, rightly struck the king as ludicrous. Having questioned Oates closely, he trapped the shameless accuser into so many lies and contradictory assertions that no kind of suspicion could possibly be attached to Queen Catherine. Instead, Oates found himself placed under house arrest on the king's orders. Yet so great was his influence that Charles was unable to intervene on behalf of Sir George, who was arrested and sent for trial.

Happily, when this took place on 18 July 1679 the accused was acquitted after a nine-hour-long hearing.

Oates' own confinement did not last longer than two or three days. Parliament, still under his spell, demanded his release, threatening dire consequences if this were not done. The celebrated rabble-rouser returned to bask in public admiration; instead of a prison cell he was allotted rooms in the Palace of Whitehall and was granted an annual pension of £1,200. The anti-Catholic brew which he had originally stirred up continued to seethe and bubble for a time, but gradually it lost its potency and subsided. As the contemporary lawyer and commentator Roger North remarked, 'the public was ... indeed tired with the blundering proceedings of Oates and his plot';[12] now Parliament and people had other things to occupy them. Yet this was not before even Samuel Pepys had been accused of 'Piracy, Popery and Treachery', locked up in the Tower of London for several weeks in some danger of a death sentence, and sacked from his influential post with the Navy on 22 May 1679, although he was reinstated in April 1684. The last person of consequence to fall victim to Oates' malign influence was the saintly Catholic Archbishop of Armagh, Oliver Plunkett, who was hideously executed at Tyburn on 1 July 1681 for high treason, defined on this occasion as 'promoting the Roman faith'.

By the end of 1678 it had become clear that Parliament, thoroughly disturbed by the Popish Plot, was actively considering measures to interfere with the succession. It had been sitting for eighteen years, and in the opinion of the king the time had come for a change. Accordingly, on 3 December he finally dissolved it, hoping that a newly-constituted House of Commons would be more ready to turn its collective mind to other matters. Charles also believed that such an outcome would be more likely if the Duke of York were not physically present in the country – a notable case of 'out of sight, out of mind'. He therefore ordered James to go abroad for a while, until the situation stabilised. Reluctantly the duke obeyed; he and the duchess left England on 3 March 1679. They first had a family reunion with William and Mary at The Hague, then moved on to Brussels where they set up their temporary home.[13] There the duke fretted the days away, receiving reports from England – some encouraging, some not – and writing numerous letters. It was a worrying time.

Back in England things were even more fraught, for all too soon the king's hopes had been dashed. After elections in February, the new Parliament assembled on 6 March, only three days after the Yorks had left the country, and soon showed itself to be even more zealously vindictive than the previous one had been. The king and his ministers had got things badly wrong; instead of a more complaisant House with a majority for the Government, they had ended up in the minority. And it is at this point in Parliamentary history that the word 'party' first assumes its modern political association, for the new Commons was clearly divided into two groups, now for the first time identified as Whigs and Tories.

'Whig' was a term originally linked with the Scottish Covenanters who in 1638 and after had opposed the religious policies of Charles I within their borders. To be a Whig therefore implied a certain measure of independence and freedom of opinion. In the 1670s and early '80s it was the Whigs who wanted an end to the threat of royal supremacy and Catholic domination. At the same time their opponents, who by and large were for maintaining the status quo and the succession, were labelled Tories. The term derives from the Irish word *toraidhe*, meaning an outlaw or robber, and was first applied derisively to the members of the group by the Whigs and their supporters, mainly because the Duke of York was known to favour the Irish.

The new House, filled with many eager new members, set to work at once. First the MPs sank their teeth metaphorically into Lord Danby, who had long been under suspicion and who now – on the basis of some letters of his to Ralph Montagu, England's former Ambassador to France – was accused of offering to make peace with the Dutch in return for a substantial sum of French money. To make matters worse, the letters were produced in the House of Commons by Montagu himself, a raffish character who had been dismissed from his post as Ambassador after some unprofessional conduct involving not only Barbara Palmer, Duchess of Cleveland, but her daughter as well. He had subsequently entered politics and become an MP – and moreover, one with a grudge against Danby whom he considered had treated him badly.[14] The Commons heard him out with glee, and then demanded Danby's arrest and impeachment for high treason. The king protested his minister's innocence to both Houses, but to no avail. On 16 April Danby was sent to the Tower.

As Roger North graphically showed, Danby had never quite got the measure of the Popish Plot brigade. 'The Earl of Danby thought he could serve himself of this plot of Oates, and accordingly endeavoured at it; but it is plain that he had no command of the engine; and … he found himself so intrigued that it was like a wolf by the ears; he could neither hold it nor let it go; and, for certain, it bit him at last: just as when a barbarous mastiff attacks a man, he cries poor cur! and is pulled down at last. So the Earl's favour did but give strength to the creature to worry him.'[15] Eventually, in the face of strenuous opposition and argument in Parliament, and after languishing in prison for five years, he was pardoned and released, but never again held office. However, he was to play an important role in the events of 1688–89, as will be shown.

For the Commons, the impeachment of Danby had been merely the *hors d'oeuvre*. The main business of the House, as the majority of MPs saw it, was to ensure the permanent exclusion of the Duke of York from the succession, and they devoted most of their sittings to this. Those who supported the cause were known, unsurprisingly, as Exclusionists. In the Lords the same theme was pursued energetically by the faction headed by Lord Shaftesbury who – despite a short truce when they had both ganged up against Danby – was by now James' implacable enemy and was widely hailed in the country at large as a doughty champion of Protestantism. His speeches in the Upper House strongly reinforced the anti-Catholic rhetoric of those in the Lower, and his dramatic delivery offset any temptation to invite ridicule. For he was hatchet-faced, his stature was notably short, and behind his back he was generally known as 'Tapski', a nickname whose bizarre origin invites explanation. Over several years he had suffered from liver trouble and in 1668 this had developed into an abscess. At the suggestion of his secretary John Locke (originally his physician), this was drained by an abdominal tube to which was fitted a small copper tap. Today the pain and hazards which must have been involved in this bold operation hardly bear thinking about, but thanks to Locke his grateful employer's life was saved.

The king, supposing that Shaftesbury's attacks were at least partly due to sour grapes, sought to blunt the savagery of those attacks by reshuffling the Council, bringing in some new opposition members, and appointing him as Lord President. But Shaftesbury was not to be mollified. Not only did he continue to support the call for Exclusion, he also impertinently suggested that the king should divorce Queen Catherine in favour of a new Protestant wife. Another proposed option was that Charles should ensure a Protestant succession by legitimising his bastard son the Duke of Monmouth. Meanwhile the Exclusion bandwagon rolled on remorselessly. On 15 May 1679 the first Exclusion Bill was passed by the Commons, and received its second reading a few days later, on 21 May. However, before it could reach the Lords the king struck back by ordering a dissolution on 3 July. So the first Exclusionist Parliament – as it became known – came to an ignominious end.

The king's problems at this time were not confined to England. In Scotland the Presbyterian faction resented the re-introduction of bishops which had been forced on them in 1660, negating the progress of Presbyterianism as Scotland's national religion and reviving painful memories of Charles I's attempts to introduce an Anglican liturgy into Scotland. These attempts had been challenged by the National Covenant of 1638, and were now being challenged again by a new generation of Covenanters. On 3 May 1679 a group of them surrounded the coach in which the Archbishop of St Andrews, James Sharp, was travelling; they dragged him out and savagely murdered him on the spot. An army of Covenanters then began to mass, and by June was sufficiently strong to defeat Government forces commanded by John Graham of Claverhouse, later 1st Viscount Dundee.

The king's answer to this threatening situation was to send the Duke of Monmouth to the north with the rank of Captain-General, to take charge of the campaign. On this occasion His Majesty's trust was not misplaced. Self-confident and full of youthful vigour, the duke trounced the Covenanters at the Battle of Bothwell Brig on 22 June.[16] Widely commended for showing an unfashionable clemency to the rebels, he was still basking in the success of his mission when on 22 August the king suddenly fell ill at Windsor with a severe fever and the spectre of the succession urgently reared its extremely ugly head.

Meanwhile in Brussels the Duke of York had been getting more and more agitated as news reached him, first, of the tactics of the Exclusionists, and then of the popularity of Monmouth following the Scottish expedition. The news of his brother's illness can only have increased his alarm, and when he received a letter from ministers advising him to return to England he lost no time in doing so. He arrived at Windsor early on the morning of 2 September, to find – no doubt to his intense relief – that the king was out of danger and recovering quickly (no thanks to his doctors, but to his own insistence on using an early form of quinine).[17] But the crisis had concentrated minds and had shown up the stark choices which were available for the succession. These were (1) James himself; (2) his elder daughter Mary (though at this stage many Exclusionists had doubts about the intentions of her husband William), or perhaps even her teenage sister Anne; (3) the Duke of Monmouth who, it was thought, might seize an opportunity to take the throne by force.

James, Duke of Monmouth (created 1663) was born in 1649 at Rotterdam, the son of the 18-year-old Prince Charles and Lucy Walter, of the same age (described by John Evelyn as 'a beautiful strumpet'). She later claimed that Charles had married her in secret, but he always strenuously denied this and in 1679 was forced to make a declaration in writing that his only legal wife was Queen Catherine.[18] In 1658 Lucy was forced to hand over James to his father, to be brought up as a member of the royal household. Of all Charles' several extra-marital children, it was James whom he loved best and who could do no wrong. Evelyn described him as 'a lovely person ... the darling of his father and the ladies, being extraordinarily handsome, and adroit: an excellent soldier & dancer, a favourite of the people [and] of an easy nature' (15 July 1685). Nell Gwynn cheekily called him 'Prince Perkin'. Rich pickings fell into his lap – the Garter, the Dukedom of Buccleuch, marriage with an heiress. His new wife was Anne (aged 12; he was 14), Countess of Buccleuch in her own right, whose family name Scott was adopted by Monmouth.[19] Meanwhile Shaftesbury worked tirelessly to promote him countrywide as 'the Protestant Duke', in clear rivalry with that other James, the Duke of York. Small wonder therefore that York regarded Monmouth with anxiety and foreboding.

Yet those who looked more closely could see the faults that lay behind Monmouth's carefree appearance. For example, he was insensitive, was lacking in *gravitas*, and had an unpleasant streak of violence which had led him, at the age of 21, to murder a night-watchman and also to organise a brutal assault on the MP Sir John Coventry, who had openly criticised the king's concubines. (A large gang of Monmouth's cronies waylaid Sir John on the street at night and forcibly removed much of his nose with a knife.)[20] Much as he loved his wayward son, Charles had no intention of letting him get anywhere near the succession; he relieved the duke of his command, and ordered him out of the country. On 24 September, a bruised and no doubt angry Monmouth wandered over to The Hague, where he poured out his woes to William and Mary.

It was clear to the king that the presence in the country of both his son and his brother, with their competing groups of supporters, was not conducive to a calm and rational consideration of the situation. Equally, to allow the Duke of York alone to remain in the country would only stir up the hornets' nest of exclusionism. James was sent back to Brussels on the day following Monmouth's departure for Holland, and in less than a month was ordered to go to Scotland.[21] He and his duchess were well received in Edinburgh, and there were no religious difficulties.

To Monmouth, the duke's absence was an opportunity too good to be missed, and to his father's great annoyance he returned to England without permission in December. 'The King was hugely surprised at his venturing to return without leave, and sends [sic] to him to be gone immediately out of the kingdom.'[22] Monmouth remained stubborn and sulkily defiant. But instead of sending him away again the king, as a counter-balance, allowed the Duke of York to return to England. The duke and duchess arrived back in London in February 1680 – but not for long. Within the space of a few months they found themselves being sent back to Scotland again, James being armed on this occasion with vice-regal powers.

The king's reasoning behind this second period of his brother's exile was that, since he must summon Parliament again (though much against his will, and then only because he needed to raise funds), it would not be a good idea to have James around when the question of the Exclusion, including even the possibility of impeachment, would almost certainly be raised. James argued and protested, even seeking the support of Louis XIV, but in vain; he left for Scotland on 20 October 1680.[23] Parliament met on the following day, and the Members at once made clear their dogged determination to pursue what Roger North called 'the battered topics of plots, exclusion, popery and the French' with a single-mindedness that allowed for little or no other business.[24] The Bill itself was read three times and then sent to the Lords – in general more sympathetic towards the king – where it was rejected by a majority of thirty-three. The acrimonious arguments continued until 10 January 1681, when the king, calling a plague on both Houses, prorogued Parliament yet again; a few days later he dissolved it and announced that it would next meet in Oxford in the spring.

Why Oxford? Charles hoped that removing MPs from the overheated atmosphere of London (where anti-Catholic mobs still roamed the streets), and more especially of Westminster, would help to focus their collective mind and introduce a more rational note into the debates. He was wrong. The new Parliament met on 21 March and the House of Commons at once showed itself to be just as unreasonable as its predecessors. After only five days the king had had enough. To the consternation of the Members he abruptly dissolved Parliament and sent them all packing. Having half expected some such development, he had taken the precaution of bringing the Crown and ceremonial robes with him to Oxford, for these regal trappings were an essential feature of any official dealings with either House. Parliament was never to be summoned again in his lifetime.

The king's surprisingly decisive move at Oxford was due in part to his sense that, in fact, given all their bluster and shouting, the Exclusionist Whigs were now actually in a weak and vulnerable position. Despite their persecution of the Duke of York they had not managed to achieve anything that might legally affect the succession. Meanwhile the continuous beating of the 'No Popery' drum, the antics of Oates and his followers, the dubious convictions, and the number and savagery of the executions had begun to weary the public. A sign of the times was the arrest on 2 July of Lord Shaftesbury, on a charge of treason. The arrest was made on the express orders of the king himself, who had long endured the Earl's various attempts to stir up the rebellious anti-Catholic Whiggish faction, both in Parliament and in the country, and now saw a chance to redress the balance. Shaftesbury was sent to the Tower, where he remained until his trial at the Old Bailey on 24 November. Owing to lack of evidence he was acquitted (to shouts of 'No Popish successor! No York! A Monmouth!'), but his opportunities to make mischief had been severely curtailed.

During Shaftesbury's time in the Tower, Titus Oates had also been experiencing some unpleasant changes. On 31 August he was ejected from his Whitehall apartment, but continued his familiar rantings against anybody whom he thought posed a 'popish' threat, including the king and the Duke of York. In the changed atmosphere of the times such dangerous impudence could no longer be tolerated. Oates was arrested and appeared briefly before Judge Jeffreys charged with sedition, for which he was heavily fined; since he was obviously unable to pay, he was immediately imprisoned. For him the good days were over. For the Duke of York, however, they had returned.

In Scotland, as the king's representative, James had done well. Mindful of Presbyterian sensibilities, he had played down his own faith and had gone out of his way to foster good relationships both on personal and on public levels. He had taken steps to improve the nation's finances and had managed to pacify the ever-volatile Highlands. Charles was pleased, and in the spring of 1682 felt confident enough of his own situation to send word that his brother might now return to England. An elated James paid a short preliminary visit during March and April, returning on 3 May to Edinburgh to wind up his affairs there and to collect his wife, who was again pregnant. On the way an unhappy incident occurred; the frigate *Gloucester*, on which the duke was travelling with his household, was wrecked through pilot error and some 200 people were drowned, noblemen, servants and sailors alike. It was alleged afterwards that the loss of life would have been considerably less, had not James insisted that a heavy strong-box, which he said contained valuable documents, should be saved above anything or anybody else. Samuel Pepys, travelling with the party, escaped danger because he had found the *Gloucester* too overcrowded for his taste and had chosen to sail in another ship, the yacht *Catherine*.[25]

The Duke and Duchess of York finally left Scotland on 15 May 1682 and in less than a fortnight had joined the king at Windsor for a short stay before taking up residence in St James's Palace. They nevertheless continued to keep close to the king when he visited his other favourite spots, especially Windsor, Winchester and Newmarket, and joined in the popular court pursuits, notably hunting (stag, fox, hare), racing and cards. The wedding of James' daughter Anne to the dull but worthy Danish Prince George, on 28 July 1683, was a notable family occasion despite the Prince's Protestant beliefs. Even the news that Monmouth was travelling round areas of the country in a travesty of a royal progress, hoping to drum up support and popularity, did not cause James much concern. It was clear that, except for parts of the West Country, which he had similarly visited in 1680, Monmouth had failed to rally a significant body of Englishmen to his cause. Moreover, his position was about to become even more precarious.

The Rye House conspiracy was hatched in the spring of 1683 (or perhaps earlier) and exposed by an informer in the following June. Its object was the assassination of both the royal brothers as they made their way back by coach to London from Newmarket, and was to have taken place near Rye House in Hertfordshire. A number of big names were implicated, and the ascendant Tories took the opportunity to get rid of several possible trouble-makers. One of the alleged plotters, the Earl of Essex, saved them the trouble by committing suicide, and there is no doubt that Shaftesbury would have come under suspicion again. But he, recognising that his power-base was gone, had fled to Amsterdam and had already died there on 21 January 1683. Nevertheless, there were others, amongst whom Lord William Russell and Algernon Sidney (great-nephew of Sir Philip, the celebrated Elizabethan soldier and poet) were considered to be the most important, and accordingly they were arrested and charged with high treason.

Sidney was a noted Republican who had held office under Cromwell but was pardoned in 1677; however, he had continued to dabble in anti-

Government politics and intrigue. He had also written an anti-authority polemic entitled *Discourses concerning Government* which, though unpublished, was to be the single most damning piece of evidence produced against him. Lord Russell was a known Whig sympathiser openly critical of the Duke of York, and had presented the Exclusion Bill in the House of Lords. Although the evidence against them was purely circumstantial and the conduct of their trials highly suspect, both were marked men and their conviction and execution were a foregone conclusion. There was, however, another high-ranking figure who was also implicated in the plot but had managed to escape arrest. This was the Duke of Monmouth.

When news of the plot leaked out Monmouth hid for a time at the country home of his mistress, Henrietta Wentworth, daughter of the Earl of Cleveland. He could easily have been found and arrested, but the king's soft-hearted attitude towards his son prevailed and Monmouth was allowed to resurface without penalty, apart from writing grovelling letters to his father and apologising to his uncle. However, he seemed subsequently to be neither sufficiently grateful nor sufficiently penitent, and the full confession which he had promised to write, containing the names of his fellow conspirators, was not forthcoming. All this infuriated his father, and in due course he skulked off in disgrace to the Netherlands where the staunchly Protestant William and Mary were only too happy to see him again. 'The prince invited him to hunt ... and at The Hague the princess paid the most marked attention to his mistress, Lady Harriet [sic] Wentworth.'[26] All this especially annoyed the Duke of York, who might have echoed the words of Macbeth, 'We have scotch'd the snake, not kill'd it', and who persuaded his more tolerant brother to make sure that all the other plotters got their just deserts.

The Rye House plot originated in the desperation of some of the more extreme Whigs as the party found its political survival coming under ever more ferocious attack by the resurgent Tories. Whigs were removed wholesale from local offices such as JPs and Deputy Lieutenants, and manoeuvred out of power in the City of London. They had no voice in Parliament which had not sat since the abortive Oxford session, and in addition many of them suffered religious persecution as the laws against Non-conformists were applied with renewed vigour.

Meanwhile the king, his ministers, the court and the Tories savoured their newfound confidence, foremost amongst them being the Duke of York. By 1684 it was almost as though all the fuss about popery and the succession, which had cost so many lives and ruined so many more, had never happened. James, it seemed, had never been closer to his brother; by the spring he was not only back in the Privy Council, but back in office as Lord High Admiral as well (in fact, though not in title).[27] More tranquil times beckoned – but never arrived. On 2 February 1685 Charles suffered the stroke which was not only to cause his death but would also completely alter the course of British history.

A Failed Rebellion

*S*o now we find ourselves back once again in that hot, airless bedroom in Whitehall, our attention centred on the tortured body of the king, weakened by the successive bleedings inflicted on him by the inept doctors who ceaselessly fussed around him. Four days had now passed since Charles had been taken ill, and although he had cheated death before, it was clear that this time he was not going to recover. The thoughts of those around him began to concentrate less on his bodily condition than on his spiritual health, to which at first he seemed strangely indifferent. An assortment of attendant bishops (London, Durham, Ely, Bath and Wells, and the Archbishop of Canterbury) urged him to take Communion and to affirm his Anglican beliefs, but he shrugged off their pleas. His soul was in jeopardy, but how could it be saved without his co-operation?

Salvation came, but from a different direction. Those around the king who were Catholic, whilst longing for a death-bed conversion, hesitated to make any over-hasty moves towards securing it, nor could such moves be initiated without the king's express permission. But eventually the Duke of York, emboldened by the certainty of his brother's impending death, and confident in the support of his duchess, the queen, and other sympathisers including Louise Kéroualle, the Duchess of Portsmouth, stepped up to the bedside and asked the king in a whisper 'if he desired he should send for a priest to him?' According to some, the king's answer was unequivocal: 'Yes, with all my heart.'[1] James' own account of what was said is somewhat different and was perhaps embroidered so as to reflect well upon himself. According to this version, to his question about the priest, the king immediately replied, 'For God's sake Brother do, and please lose no time.' He then added: 'But will you not expose yourself too much by doing it? The Duke ... answer'd, Sir, tho' it cost me my life I will bring one to you.'[2]

Despite the recent religious upheavals Whitehall was not short of Catholic priests. A Portuguese contingent was attached to the queen's household, an Italian one to that of Mary of Modena. But few if any of them spoke English, and to invite any one of them into the king's bedroom would have been a huge public relations disaster, as James was well aware. It would have cancelled out all the good work that had been done recently to take the spotlight off his own Catholicism and to restore his credentials as heir to the throne. However, as it happened a solution to the problem was most conveniently to hand in the person of Father Huddleston.

John Huddleston was a Lancashire man born near Preston in 1608, a Catholic who had joined the Benedictine order. In 1651 he was acting as family tutor at Moseley Hall near Boscobel House in Shropshire, and had helped to conceal the young King Charles at Moseley after the disastrous defeat at Worcester. (The king, dressed as a woodman, with dirty face and hands and with hair hacked short by a knife, had already spent a day sheltering in the famous Boscobel oak – a story which he never tired of telling, as his courtiers could confirm only too well.)[3] At the Restoration Charles showed his gratitude to Father Huddleston by giving him shelter at court, where he was attached successively to the households of the Queen Mother Henrietta Maria, and of Queen Catherine of Braganza. From about 1670 the priest had been living in some secrecy in Whitehall and was not known to many.[4] Now, having received the summons to attend the dying king, it was more than ever essential that his identity should be concealed.

So it was in the garb of an Anglican cleric and wearing an incongruous black wig that the good Father hurriedly followed the messenger along the labyrinthine galleries and passages of the palace until, by way of a secret entrance, he reached the royal apartments. Here he waited in an anteroom while the Duke of York cleared the bedroom of all onlookers and hangers-on, until only the duke himself and two Protestant but trustworthy noblemen – the earls of Bath and Feversham – remained. Then at last Father Huddleston was admitted into the presence of the dying monarch. He stood in the shadows as the duke, bending down over his brother, said: 'Sire, here is a man that saved your life, and is now come to save your soul.' The response, though spoken in a whisper, was firm and immediate: 'He is very welcome.'[5]

Charles indeed received the priest gratefully, recognising that now, at the very end, he had reached that spiritual goal for which his soul had secretly yearned during much of his adult life. In answer to Father Huddleston's formal questions he affirmed his Catholic faith and made his confession; the priest then gave him absolution and Extreme Unction (anointing of the dying with holy oil), and finally administered the sacrament of Communion. John Huddleston then left the room in tears, his work done. No sooner had he gone than the ghoulish crowd waiting outside were re-admitted to witness their king's rapidly approaching end. To those nearest to him, but especially to his brother James, he commended his wife, his mistresses (particularly Louise de Kérouaille and Nell Gwynn), and all his children – except the disgraced Monmouth, whom he did not mention. After ordering the curtains to be drawn back, he then sank gradually into a coma as the early morning light flooded into the room.

Charles II died at noon on that same day, Friday 6 February 1685. While those around him were not privy to what had gone on in his bedroom for the short time (about an hour) during which they had been ousted from it, suspicions had earlier been aroused by his refusal to take Communion from his Anglican chaplains, and it was not long before rumours began to circulate, as John Evelyn noted: 'Others whispered, that the Bishops being bid withdraw ... Hurlston [sic] the Priest had presum'd to administer the popish Offices; I hope it is not true.' However, now was not the time to confront such rumours, but rather to concentrate on new beginnings.

Once it had become known that the king was very probably dying, a general sense of unreality seems to have prevailed. There was also some fear for, given the events of the past few years, nobody knew what would happen next. Roger North and his brother Dudley, a City merchant, were themselves deeply affected: 'We walked about like ghosts, generally to and from Whitehall. We met few persons without passion in their eyes, as we also had. We thought of no concerns, public or private, but were contented to live and breathe as if we had nought else to do but to expect the issue of this grand crisis.'[6] (A similar atmosphere seems to have gripped London during the Abdication furore of 1936.) Had it happened a few years earlier, the same crisis might have led to unrest and violence on the streets; now, however, the national mood had changed. As Roger reported: 'It pleased God that the temper of the nation was at this time so universally settled in loyalty (saving only the very dregs of a malevolent party) that there was no apprehension of any disorder either during the King's sickness or after his decease; but, on the contrary, almost every living soul cried before and at his decease as for the loss of the best friend in the world.'[7]

When the end came at last, the tempo of events changed rapidly with the proclamation of the new king's succession, witnessed by the two North brothers from the roof of Inigo Jones' Banqueting House. From their vantage point they watched the emerging procession, 'being persons of quality and heralds mounted who, after drums and trumpets, made the proclamation … And we two on the top of the balusters were the first that gave the shout, and signal with our hats for the rest to shout, which was followed sufficiently.'[8] The proclamation was actually made at the so-called Holbein Gate, a decorative Tudor structure which stood at right-angles to the Banqueting House but which in fact had no connection with the famous artist whose name it bore. It was demolished in 1759.

After the ceremony, the procession moved on to Temple Bar and thence to the Exchange in Cornhill (the proclamation being repeated at each stop), before returning to Whitehall Palace. Here the participants were ushered into the presence of their new king, who had managed to snatch a few hours' rest after his exhausting ordeal – 'tired indeede as he was with grief & watching,' as John Evelyn put it. They were also received by the new Queen Mary. Evelyn, who had formed part of the entourage, gave a graphic and rather touching account of this meeting:

> Being come to Whitehall, we all went and kissed the King & Queenes
> hands; he had ben on the bed, but was now risen, & in his Undresse. The

Queene was in bed in her apartment, but put forth her hand; seeming to be much afflicted, as I believe she was, having deported herselfe so decently upon all occasions since she came first into England, which made her universally beloved [6 February 1685].

Refreshed and reinvigorated, James now held an impromptu meeting of the Privy Council at which, in a speech delivered without notes, he promised 'to preserve the Government in Church and State as it is now by law established' – a promise which concealed his unspoken intention to introduce parallel advantages for Catholicism in every stratum of society.[9] But for the time being he was careful not to overstep the mark, although he made no attempt to conceal his own faith. On the contrary, John Evelyn reported that on Sunday 8 February he 'did now [for] the first time go to Masse publicly in the little Oratorie at the Duke's lodgings, the doores set wide open' – so that everybody could see him clearly. The gesture was intended as one of reassurance, showing the populace that their new king, while ready to protect their rights, was nevertheless a man of principle. In James' memoirs the chapel is further identified as 'the little Chappel in St. James's' and must surely refer to the queen's chapel in the precincts of St James's Palace.[10] The chapel's doors conveniently open directly onto the footpath. Built by Inigo Jones and not so little, it was begun in 1623 at a time when Charles I, as Prince of Wales, was expected to marry a Spanish princess, and was completed by 1625, by which time Charles had instead married Henrietta Maria of France. Thus, since its foundation, the chapel had always been set aside for Catholic worship.

In contrast to James' very public profession of his personal faith, made in the full light of day, the funeral of his late royal brother took place on 14 February in the south aisle of Henry VII's Chapel, Westminster Abbey, at the dead hour of midnight. This might seem a strange kind of leave-taking of a monarch who for the most part had been in his day genuinely beloved by his people, but in fact it was not so unusual. (On 21 September 1660 Samuel Pepys saw the coffin of the Duke of Gloucester taken by water from Somerset House to Westminster, 'to be buried tonight'.) In any case the funeral had been preceded by a ceremonial lying-in-state in Whitehall, at which a life-size wax effigy of the late king, standing and dressed in Garter robes, presided over the occasion. It is still preserved in the collection of such figures at the Abbey, and its height – 6ft 2in – is a reminder that for those days Charles was exceptionally tall. The funeral itself was conducted with due solemnity and some splendour, despite the overwhelming display of black, whether in costumes or hangings, and was attended by a number of noblemen and high-ranking dignitaries, though apparently not by James. His absence, which might also be considered unusual, was in fact due to contemporary custom which dictated that the closest relative to a deceased was not present at the burial.[11]

Surprisingly, John Evelyn (who should have known better) gave a garbled account of the event which to this day has misled many people: 'The King was very obscurely buried in a Vault under Hen[ry] 7th Chapell in Westminster, without any manner of pomp' (*Diary*, 14 February 1685). But in another strange twist of fortune, the outwardly genial and popular Charles II, known familiarly to the man in the street as 'Old Rowley' (originally the name of one of the king's favourite stallions), was given no public monument other than a small stone tablet which is set into the floor of the Chapel, marking the site of the burial vault, and which records only his name.

The funeral over, public attention now concentrated on the next ceremonial occasion – the coronation. The date was fixed for 23 April, St George's Day, a symbolic date perhaps chosen to emphasise James' reassuring Englishness. This gave time for the necessary preparations to be made, including the erection of spectators' galleries within Westminster Abbey and for the building of the central enthronement platform at the crossing of the nave and transepts. When the day itself came, a sequence of colourful and stately processions was made from Westminster Hall to the Abbey, in which the coronation ritual was presided over by the Archbishop of Canterbury, William Sancroft, and the Dean of Westminster, Thomas Sprat (who was also Bishop of Rochester).

The order of service, drawn up by Sancroft, mainly followed that used at the coronation of Charles I, with one important exception – in deference to James' Catholicism the Communion, usually the very heart of the service, was omitted. To make up for this the general splendour of the ritual was emphasised, especially in the music which was supplied by five different composers. These were William Child, Henry Lawes, William Turner, John Blow and the great Henry Purcell. At the time all were still living except Lawes, who had died in 1662. Today the first three are little remembered – perhaps unjustly – except by specialists and those interested in so-called 'early music'. Blow was a considerable composer whose works are still sometimes performed, but he is inevitably overshadowed by his former pupil Purcell, whom he highly respected. At the time of the 1685 coronation Purcell was Keeper of the King's Instruments, organist of the Chapel Royal, and organist of Westminster Abbey – a post which the aptly named Blow had relinquished in his favour in 1679, and was to resume after Purcell's death. Purcell's chief contribution to the coronation music was his sublime eight-part anthem, *My heart is inditing*. (The same text was used again by Handel in one of his four well-known anthems written for the coronation of George II.)

It was at James' coronation that the Abbey rang for the first time with the acclamation 'Vivat Rex' shouted out by the Westminster scholars. While this has become a tradition since the coronation of Edward VII (1902), it was perhaps originally introduced as a cover for any embarrassing silence that might have greeted James.

'THE FAMOUS MR HENRY PURCELL'

At the time of James II's coronation Henry Purcell (b. 1659) was 26 years old. A former Chapel Royal chorister who came of a musical family, he had already been organist of Westminster Abbey for six years and, simultaneously, of the Chapel Royal for three. In this capacity he began to compose the sequence of anthems which are his distinctive contribution to the Anglican liturgy of his day. Most were written during the reign of Charles II, often with instrumental accompaniment, in line with the French taste which Charles himself had absorbed whilst in exile. Amongst the last and the greatest was *My heart is inditing*, composed expressly for the coronation of James II (see main text).

However, Purcell was far from being only a church musician. After the Revolution religious music was in temporary decline; thus much of his work in the 1690s was for the theatre, in the form of overtures and incidental music ('curtain tunes') for plays such as *The Gordian Knot Unty'd* and *Abdelazer*. From this time also came the 'semi-operas' – that is, spoken drama carried forward by operatic-style arias and other musical interludes, a peculiarly English tradition. These included *King Arthur* (1691, words by Dryden), *The Fairy-Queen* (1692, based on *A Midsummer Night's Dream*) and *The Indian Queen* (1695). But Purcell had already surpassed them in 1689 with *Dido and Aeneas*, which is sung throughout; as such it ranks, to all intents and purposes, as the first true English opera and is still performed today. It is usually said to have been first performed at a girls' school in Chelsea, although there is now some evidence that it may have appeared somewhat earlier, perhaps as an entertainment at court.

Purcell changed the direction of English musical taste from the French style, which was essentially dance-oriented, lightweight and predictable, to the Italian, which was new in its forms and more thoughtful in its construction. He signalled his intentions in the preface to his first printed composition, a set of twelve instrumental pieces entitled *Sonnata's of III Parts*, in which he castigated 'the levity and balladry of our neighbours' [i.e. the French] and stated that he had 'faithfully endeavour'd a just imitation of the most fam'd Italian masters [so as] to bring the seriousness and gravity of that sort of musick into vogue and reputation among our countrymen'. However, it seems that seriousness and gravity were not notably part of his own character. For his friends and other social circles he wrote the music for a number of catches or part-songs, some of which are set to texts whose bawdy content would make even today's permissive society blush.

Purcell's first task for William and Mary was to organise the music for their coronation. Owing to their lack of enthusiasm for pomp and circumstance, the ceremony itself was less sumptuous than it had been for James, and Purcell sensibly re-used one of the anthems he had provided for that occasion, *I was glad*. But he also rose to the challenge and wrote a new anthem, *Praise the Lord O Jerusalem*, which immediately followed the actual crowning and (perhaps in deference to William's austere taste) is somewhat less flamboyant than the magnificent *My heart is inditing* of 1685.

In the 1680s Purcell had begun a series of Odes celebrating royal birthdays and other occasions, such as welcoming King Charles back to Whitehall after the summer recess or the Duke of York's return from Scotland in 1682. Each Ode consisted of an appropriate poem dressed up in a sequence of choruses, solo arias and instrumental pieces, much of the music being of high quality. Unfortunately the same cannot be said of the poems, whose general banality and nauseous flattery is the main reason why most of the Odes – sometimes alternatively called Welcome Songs – are seldom if ever publicly performed today. With the arrival of William and Mary a different kind of Ode took their place. The new queen's birthday fell on 30 April, a bare three weeks after the coronation, but despite the short time available Purcell was nevertheless expected to provide a celebratory piece. He rose magnificently to the occasion with *Now does the glorious day appear* (words by Thomas Shadwell), a work in the tradition and format of the Odes, but which in its wealth of rich musical invention and opulent string accompaniment far surpassed anything he had so far produced in this genre. It proved to be the first of six Birthday Odes which he was to write for Mary, culminating in the finest of them all, *Come, ye sons of art, away* (1694, words anonymous). In it the listeners are urged to *Sing your patronesses praise / In cheerful and harmonious lays* – a tribute to the queen, who had shown a genuine interest in the arts and it seems had developed as friendly a relationship with Purcell as she had with Wren.

Come ye sons of art was the last Birthday Ode that Purcell was to compose for his queen. Seven months later she was dead. Like Wren, Purcell used his art as an expression of his personal sense of loss, composing some of the most poignant funeral music ever written. The emotive simplicity of the short choral movements sung in the Abbey is mirrored in the solemn march for the group of brass instruments which preceded the hearse in the funeral procession.

Almost a year later, the same music was heard again at another funeral which took place in the Abbey – Purcell's own. 'The famous Mr Henry Purcell' (as he was hailed) died, it seems unexpectedly, on 21 November 1695, to the great grief of all who had known him personally and many who knew him only through his music. As a mark of regard and respect the Abbey authorities granted him a free burial in the north aisle, where his epitaph assures us that he 'is gone to that blessed place where only his harmony can be exceeded'.

It might be thought strange that, apart from the Communion, James was apparently so willing to conform to the traditions of the Anglican ritual, including his own crowning. However, it seems he had already taken out a form of spiritual insurance on the day before, by having himself and the queen anointed and crowned in the Whitehall chapel according to Catholic precepts. In the Abbey the crown at one point slipped lopsidedly on his head, an unfortunate mishap which inevitably was seen as a bad omen. Nor was it the only one. The antiquarian John Aubrey reported that, 'The canopy carried over King James II's head by the Wardens of the Cinque Ports was torn by a puff of wind as he came to Westminster Hall. It hung down very lamentably; I saw it. 'Twas of cloth of gold and my strength (I am confident) could not have rent it and it was not a windy day. The top of his sceptre ... did then fall, which the Earl of Peterborough took up.'[12]

Happier memories of the ceremony still remain today, in the shapes of the Coronation Crown, 'Diadem' or ceremonial cap, Sceptre and Ivory Rod, all specially made for and used by Mary of Modena on that occasion. All these items remain with the royal regalia in the Tower of London, except for the Coronation Crown (since greatly altered) which is in the Museum of London. Also amongst the Crown Jewels in the Tower is Mary's State Crown, made for her by the jeweller Richard de Beauvoir.[13]

According to custom the coronation service was followed by a huge state banquet held in Westminster Hall, at which over 1,000 dishes were served while privileged onlookers surveyed the scene enviously from specially erected galleries. During the proceedings the archaically armoured King's Champion (since 1377 always a member of the Dymoke family) rode into the Hall on a charger and, in accordance with tradition, challenged to single combat any malcontents disposed to argue against the new monarch's authority. Our in-depth knowledge of the occasion, and indeed of the coronation service itself, owes much to Francis Sandford, a genealogist and herald who recorded the events in a series of meticulously detailed engravings with accompanying text which he published in 1687 as *The History of the Coronation of the Most High, Most Mighty, and Most Excellent Monarch, James II*. He shows the settings and ceremonies in the Abbey, the various people taking part in the processions, the feast (listing its gargantuan menu) and many other features. Indeed, before the arrival of photography no other English coronation received such exhaustive pictorial coverage. Sadly for Sandford, however, the book came out too late to capitalise on James' then waning popularity; it failed to make a profit, and the author ended his days in a debtors' prison. The festivities themselves ended rather more splendidly with a tremendous fireworks display on the Thames, which had to be postponed to the following evening because James and his queen were exhausted by all the ceremonial.[14] However, it seems that even this presaged disaster. Aubrey reported that the assorted rockets, Roman candles and Catherine wheels 'took fire all together, and it was so dreadful that several spectators leap'd into the river, choosing rather to be drown'd than burn'd'.

In the interval between his brother's death and his own coronation James had taken steps to call elections for a new Parliament. It is worth recalling that Parliamentary elections at this period had very little to do with modern ideas of democracy. A prospective MP was carefully chosen by a patron – a nobleman, a landowner, a collective body, or in some instances the Crown itself – who then presented him to the comparatively few citizens who were actually entitled to vote. In his later years Charles II and his ministers had engineered significant changes to the charters of a number of boroughs and town councils, so that their make-up would be tilted towards Tory majorities and their choice of MP influenced accordingly. Unsurprisingly therefore, and to James' pleasure, the make-up of the new House of Commons reflected general satisfaction over his succession, despite all that had gone before, and a corresponding swing against the exclusionist, no-Popery attitude of the recent past. Out of the total number of 513 seats, only 57 had been taken by Whigs, the rest going to the Tories.[15] As for the inner circle of Charles' ministers – which included the earls of Halifax, Sunderland, Middleton and Arlington – James kept them all on, though some of the posts were redistributed.

A typical example of a Tory 'placeman' was Roger North's brother Dudley, whose selection by the king's advisors as MP for Banbury was based solely on his standing and experience as a businessman. Although entirely a stranger to Parliament and its workings, he 'took the place of manager for the Crown in all matters of revenue stirring in the House of Commons'. Those who had hand-picked him as a Government spokesman found their choice entirely vindicated, for 'what he undertook he carried through against all opposition, with as much assurance and dexterity as if he had been an old battered Parliament-man'.[16] However, not all the new members were so enthusiastic or assiduous, 'very many … being divers of them persons of no manner or condition or interest in the nation,' as Evelyn remarked (22 May 1685).

Parliament assembled on 24 May, both Houses by tradition crowding into the Lords to hear the king's speech. (At the time, and until the early nineteenth century, the Lords met in a large room within the Palace of Whitehall, called the Queen's Chamber.) In his speech, James repeated the promises he had made to the Privy Council on 6 February, notably that he would preserve the privileges of the Church of England and the rights of individual subjects. He then brought up the all-important topic of money, asking that in the interests of prudent financial planning the Commons should settle on him a revenue for life. This, he pointed out, would be far preferable to their voting periodic piecemeal handouts, a method which it seemed some MPs would prefer. There followed a veiled threat whose smooth delivery obscured its ruthless content: 'This would be a very improper method to take with me, and … the best way to engage me to meet you often is always to use me well. I expect you will comply with me in what I have desired, and that you will do it speedily, that this may be a short session and that we may soon meet again to all our satisfactions.'[17]

Any slight doubts that might have been aroused by these words were soon stifled by different emotions as James went on to conclude the speech by announcing some important news just received. This was, that a disaffected Scots nobleman, the Earl of Argyll, had recently landed in the Orkneys from the Netherlands with a band of armed followers and was busy fomenting rebellion, disputing James' right to the throne. Argyll's treasonable activities stemmed from his reluctance to swear the oath of loyalty to the Crown during the period of James' vice-regal rule in Scotland. Charged with treason, he had been tried and convicted in Edinburgh, but had managed to escape from imprisonment in the Castle (dressed as his daughter's footman) and to flee overseas.[18]

News of Argyll's incursion raised Parliament to a fever pitch of enthusiastic patriotism and the chamber rang with shouts of *Vive le Roi* which must have been music to James' ears. Only one person failed to share in the general rejoicing; this was Francis North, Baron Guilford, Keeper of the Great Seal (in effect, Lord Chancellor) and elder brother of Dudley and Roger North. He had expected to be invited, by tradition, to give a loyal address after the king had spoken, and accordingly had prepared an appropriate speech – strong, measured and respectful toward the new monarch: 'Never therefore let our Church of England fear to want support when he hath said he will defend it. Never let any man entertain the least jealousy of arbitrary government, when his Majesty hath declared against it.'[19] But the royal invitation to speak did not come and the king left the chamber without further ceremony. This may have been an oversight; on the other hand it may well have been a deliberate snub aimed at one whom James had lately come to regard as unsound, mistaking Lord Guilford's cautious impartiality for deliberate obstruction. Significantly, Evelyn reported that 'It was whispered, he would not be long in that station.'

This incident illustrates the less attractive side of James' personality. On the plus side he was honest, industrious, fundamentally well-meaning and, within the conventions of the age, not without conscience. While this last aspect of his character had not been much in evidence in the past, now, in the interests of good public relations, the time had come to present a new face to the country. Although he kept a mistress – Catherine Sedley, later created Countess of Dorchester – she was now banished from court. However, she soon returned and the liaison continued more or less openly until the queen had had enough. 'She upbraided her husband with his infidelity; she declared that she would withdraw to a convent … and it was remarked that on two successive days at dinner she neither ate, nor uttered a word to the king.' Gathering about herself a group of powerful Catholic noblemen and clergy, she prepared an ambush for her husband. A dramatic confrontation then took place. 'When James entered to visit the queen, he was instantly assailed by their united remonstrances against an attachment so injurious to his consort, so disgraceful to his religion, and so prejudicial to his own interest. He was surprised, abashed, and subdued' (and no wonder).[20] Although this was not entirely the end of the affair it was subsequently conducted with much greater caution.

Drunkenness, swearing, duelling and gambling, essential features of court life under Charles II, were now frowned upon, and theatre audiences were specifically taken to task for their unruly behaviour.[21] (This above all was perhaps the thing which led the irrepressibly saucy ex-actress Nell Gwynn to christen James 'Dismal Jimmy'.) Against the basically good if boring qualities must be set the minus tally, for James was also proud, humourless, tactless, narrow-minded and obstinate. Nor was he one to forgive those whom he believed had wronged him, amongst whom one of the most prominent was Titus Oates.

With the passage of time, and especially with all the euphoria surrounding the accession of the new king, the name of the obnoxious Oates had been largely forgotten – but not by James. On his specific instructions Oates was brought from Newgate gaol to Westminster Hall on 7 May to face a re-trial for perjury, and on 16 May was sentenced to life imprisonment, an annual appearance in the pillory at five different locations in London, and severe corporal punishment in the form of a public whipping at the cart's tail. He was also forbidden to wear clerical dress. So far had Oates sunk in public esteem that his appearance in the pillory (an experience that had been known to prove fatal for some) probably attracted more than the usual hail of ordure, eggs, mud, sticks, stones and other missiles, although he seems to have escaped serious injury. The whipping took place over two different routes on two different days, one of these routes being from Aldgate to Newgate (Wednesday). On the other, from Newgate to Tyburn (Friday), Oates endured the punishment whilst being dragged through the streets on a hurdle, as he was too weak from the previous scourging to walk behind the cart.[22]

The vindictive if well-deserved treatment of Oates, like the king's speech at the opening of Parliament, may have caused some of the more thoughtful MPs to reflect on what the future might hold for the country. For the most part, however, the Commons returned to their chamber to conduct a loyal debate on the subject of the king's financial needs. Despite misgivings on the part of some Members, the House (with its built-in Tory majority and keen to keep on the right side of the new monarch) resolved 'that the revenue which was settled on his late Majesty for his life, be settled on his present Majesty for his life', the said revenue amounting to an annual grant of £1,200,000.[23] In normal circumstances this might have satisfied James, at least for a time. However, Argyll's northern rebellion had put a different complexion on things, and on 30 May the king came back to Parliament for more. Extra funds were needed, he said, to supply his forces and to finance the campaign, as well as to pay off additional debts left by his late brother. It seemed that new taxes would have to be raised.

The task of finding out how this was best to be done fell to Dudley North. After much deliberation, 'he thought fit to propose a tax of one farthing upon sugars and one halfpenny upon tobacco imported ... and this, as he estimated, would yield the sum expected, and would scarce be any burthen sensible to the people.'[24] Many a modern Chancellor of the Exchequer has had similar ideas. Dudley's proposal was adopted with enthusiasm, and despite some opposition from the usual vested interests (mainly tradesmen) a Bill was drawn up, debated and passed. Extra revenue was secured by a Bill allowing the import of French wines and vinegar (which formerly had been banned), thus increasing the revenue from Customs. These arrangements were scheduled to last for a period of eight years, and were expected to raise £400,000 annually.[25] But more was to come. The month of June had hardly begun before MPs were voting to give the king another £400,000, also raised from duties (on linen, silks and spirits) and this time for a period of five years. The royal coffers were now filled to the tune of £2m or more, making James II the first financially independent English monarch – and, as such, a possible threat to Parliament itself. Why then were MPs so generous towards him and, in particular, what had prompted the second vote of £400,000? The answer lay in some alarming news that had arrived in London on 13 June. The Duke of Monmouth had landed at Lyme Regis in Dorset on 11 June and had raised the standard of rebellion against his uncle.

In fact Monmouth's unwelcome arrival was the second part of what was to have been a two-pronged attack, the first being Argyll's Scottish adventure. The plan had been hatched in the Netherlands – seething with disaffected and exiled Whigs – as a result of collusion between the two arch-rebels and their followers, and relied for its success on the element of surprise and also on the wide distance between the two points of attack. It seems that William of Orange, while officially aligning himself with James and keeping him informed about Monmouth's activities, tacitly supported the rebels by giving them access to ships and weaponry. His hope may well have been, not so much that Monmouth would be successful, but rather that the plan would fail and that he would be defeated, thus confirming William's wife Mary as the sole undoubted heir to her father's throne.

The plan did indeed fail, partly through lack of co-ordination. Argyll left Amsterdam for Scotland on 2 May, but, once arrived, his small ragtag army (which included members of his own clan Campbell) was soon pursued and scattered, while he himself was caught at Inchinnan near Glasgow on 18 June. Recruits had not flocked to his banner as he had hoped, and there had been little general enthusiasm for his cause.[26] On the other hand Monmouth, delayed by the weather, was unable to sail for England until 30 May, so that by the time he actually landed Argyll was in full retreat. The earl was arrested a week later and swiftly executed.

As a force, Monmouth's invading army, like that of Argyll, was less than impressive, estimates of its size varying from the low eighties to about one hundred and fifty. The duke, however, was confident that in the West Country, which had welcomed him so warmly during his semi-royal progress through its towns and villages back in 1680, he would find enough volunteers to form the nucleus of a formidable army. Once on the march (he believed), this army would gather up new recruits as it went along; opposition would melt away, and he would enter London to general acclamation.

First results seemed to vindicate his optimism. In a rousing, rambling proclamation issued on landing, he accused his uncle James – whom he continued to call the Duke of York – of a long list of crimes including tyranny and murder (even of poisoning Charles II), branded him as a usurper, a traitor and a papist, and pledged that the rebellion would reform Parliament, repeal unjust legislation, and generally put things right. In return he received from the population of Lyme the rapturous welcome for which he had hoped; recruitment began, and was continued along the route through Dorset and Somerset, but on the whole it failed to produce the kind of manpower which was needed. Above all, there was a lack of officer material, for many of the local gentry on whom Monmouth had hoped to rely, while perhaps privately sympathising with his aims, showed a marked reluctance to get involved with the campaign. (Amongst the few notable people to join the cause as a Dissenter was a merchant, Daniel Defoe, who many years later would become known as the author of *Robinson Crusoe*.) As for Monmouth's foot-soldiers, their ranks were formed mainly from artisans, peasants, seamen and miners from the Mendip hills, many of them Dissenters and Non-conformists bound together by a common fear of popery which, they believed, threatened their own liberal religious beliefs. Their weapons – scythes, billhooks, pitchforks, some musketry – were woefully inadequate, their numbers persistently low, probably somewhere between 3,000 and 4,000, but their enthusiasm (at least to begin with) made up for these deficiencies as they threw up their caps and shouted heartily for 'King Monmouth!'

Despite the efforts of the local part-time militia to disrupt its progress, the rebel army now headed for Bristol, which it hoped to attack. However, it was already being shadowed by a small but formidable body of infantry (five companies), backed up by cavalry (eight troops) and led by Brigadier John Churchill, the future Duke of Marlborough.[27] The overall commander-in-chief sent from London to take charge of events was Louis Duras, Earl of Feversham, who though originally a French Huguenot refugee had in the eyes of King James the great advantage of also being the nephew of James' great hero and friend Marshal Turenne. Slow to act and indecisive, he was not a military genius of the calibre of his uncle and certainly not of Churchill who was now about to show signs of that sense of purpose, initiative and grasp of essentials which were to carry him forward to greater things, and who was the real brains behind the Government campaign. However, on this occasion a sophisticated battle-plan was not necessary, for the king's generals already had two important advantages over the rebels – a force greatly superior in training if not in numbers, and the weather. Heavy rain put paid to Monmouth's designs on Bristol, and the rebel army disconsolately retraced its steps via Frome, Shepton Mallet and Wells to Bridgwater.

Soaked to the skin and footsore, Monmouth's men nonetheless kept faith with their leader, and indeed they had nobody else to turn to. Desertion was not an option, for it was known that such stragglers as had been rounded up earlier by Lord Feversham's men had been hanged out of hand and that no mercy could be expected from that quarter. An offer from the king to pardon those who surrendered within eight days was treated with suspicion and scepticism. What was <u>not</u> known, was that Monmouth himself had begun to lose heart and apparently had seriously thought of creeping back secretly to the Netherlands, leaving his army in the lurch.[28] But instead, he was galvanised into a last, frenzied effort by the news that the king's army had made camp at Sedgemoor, near Bridgewater. A successful surprise attack on the camp by night could, it was thought, tip the balance back in the duke's favour. At least it was worth a try.

On 6 July, in the half-darkness and swirls of early morning mist, the weary but tense rebels crept through the undergrowth and crossed water-filled ditches, known in Somerset as rhines. As they tried to ford the largest of these, Langmoor Rhine, one of them took fright at a shadow and – disobeying Monmouth's express order – fired at it, shattering the silence. In that moment the battle was lost. The king's men were momentarily taken off guard, but their superior training and discipline soon began to tell. In the ragged ranks of Monmouth's army a trickle of demoralised deserters soon became a rout, pursued by Churchill's avenging cavalry. Some fugitives were shot in the ditches where they lay in hiding, others were dragged out and summarily hanged. Many more were taken prisoner and thrown into local gaols to await their fate. All too often that fate was to be embodied in the terrifying figure of the infamous Judge Jeffreys.

George Jeffreys was born at Acton near Wrexham in 1648, took to the law, and was called to the Bar in 1668. His career prospered; he became solicitor to the then Duke of York, received a knighthood in 1677, became Recorder of London in 1678 and Chief Justice of the King's Bench in 1683. He presided over the trials of the Rye House plotter, Algernon Sidney, and of Titus Oates. Roger North had many opportunities to see Jeffreys in action and recorded his impressions of the Chief Justice: 'When he was in temper and matters indifferent came before him, he became his seat of justice better than any other I ever saw in his place. He took a pleasure in mortifying fraudulent attorneys and would deal forth his severities with a sort of majesty.'[29] Bold and self-confident, he exuded what John Evelyn called 'an assured and undaunted spirit'.

There was, however, another side to Jeffreys: 'His delights were ... drinking, laughing, singing, kissing, and all the extravagances of the bottle ... Many times ... the company have waited five hours in a morning, and after eleven, he hath come out inflamed and staring like one distracted.' Such 'mornings after' did little to improve his temper. 'His weakness was that he could not reprehend without scolding, and in such Billingsgate language as should not come out of the mouth of any man. He called it "giving a lick with the rough side of his tongue". It was ordinary to hear him say, *Go, you are a filthy, lousy, knitty rascal*, with much more of like elegance.'[30] Even when sober he would habitually browbeat and intimidate witnesses.[31] He is sometimes said to have been the model for Judge Hate-Good in John Bunyan's *Pilgrim's Progress* (1678). Although there was certainly more to Jeffreys than his reputation as a foul-mouthed inebriate would suggest, it is undoubtedly the side of his character which is best remembered today.

Ruthlessly ambitious, and with his eye fixed firmly on the Lord Chancellorship, Jeffreys connived with the Earl of Sunderland to denigrate the work and character of Francis North, Lord Guilford, at every opportunity, openly insulting him and suggesting to the king that the Lord Keeper was (in a well-known twentieth-century phrase) 'not one of us' – something which James had already suspected for some time. Conversely he appreciated Jeffrey's undoubted loyalty, and was prepared to overlook one of the Chief Justice's few claims to honesty, which was his refusal to abandon his Protestant beliefs. When therefore the king selected Jeffreys as his agent of justice in the West Country, he did so in the knowledge that there would be no hesitation in meting out the kind of severe royal retribution that he had in mind for the rebels and their associates.

Towards the end of August Jeffreys, together with four colleagues, arrived in the West Country, armed with the king's commission (the quaintly named Oyer and Terminer) to hold special assizes. There were fewer cases to deal with than there might have been, since a number of the original prisoners had died as a result of being kept for over a month in the hot, crowded, fever-ridden and insanitary conditions prevailing in the various small county gaols into which they had been herded. The principal towns where the trials were held were Exeter, Salisbury, Dorchester, Taunton and Wells. At Dorchester Jeffreys is said to have lodged at No. 6 High West Street, the trials being held in what is now the Oak Room of the Antelope Hotel. At Taunton the setting was the Great Hall of the Castle, now the County Museum.

In court Jeffreys bullied and blustered his way through the various cases in his usual hectoring manner, wasting little time on formalities and totally dominating the proceedings. A few of the rebels were pardoned, including Daniel Defoe, who escaped to London before the troops caught him (he later became an advisor, probably also a spy, for King William). But for most of those brought before the courts (said to number over 1,000) there was only one sentence – death. In practice only about 300 were actually executed, the remainder having their sentences commuted to transportation. The majority of those executed were not only hanged, but drawn and quartered as well, their body parts being distributed throughout the towns and villages of the area as a dreadful warning. Not for nothing did this episode come to be known as the Bloody Assizes. It was and remains the chief event for which Jeffreys is remembered, and nowhere, even today, with more visceral hatred than in the West Country.

In London there were those who thought that Jeffreys had gone too far and that there had been too much bloodshed. Not so King James (although he was later to try to distance himself from the carnage, blaming Jeffreys for 'an excess of zeal').[32] So far as he was concerned, the Chief Justice had done precisely what was expected of him and had once again proved his unswerving loyalty to the Crown. It was therefore with grim satisfaction that James welcomed Jeffreys back from the West Country and was able to bestow on him the Lord Chancellorship which he had long craved, for Lord Guilford (worn out by the cares of his office and the venomous attacks of his political enemies including Jeffreys) had died while the infamous assizes were in progress. For good measure James also elevated Jeffreys to the peerage with the title of Baron Jeffreys of Wem in the county of Shropshire.

Meanwhile, what of Monmouth? By the time the trials began he had been already dead for over a month. Having fled the field at Sedgemoor, he survived for three days as a fugitive, only to be found by troopers hiding in a ditch, with a pocketful of dried peas for sustenance. He was taken back to London, where he begged desperately in letters for an interview with his uncle. James reluctantly agreed, but the sight of his nephew shamelessly grovelling before him and pleading for mercy did nothing to placate him. Not one to forgive or forget, he was not about to pardon a rebellious subject who had caused him so much unease in the past, even though they might be closely related. Monmouth was condemned out of hand under the terms of the original Act passed against him *in absentia* after the Rye House plot; no further trial was needed. On 15 July, two days after his painful interview with the king, he was beheaded on Tower Hill by an inexpert executioner who bungled the job and had to deliver five blows to complete it, to the fury of the crowd.

Some of the bigger names implicated directly in the rebellion or in the Rye House plot were either imprisoned for short periods and pardoned, or got off with large fines, such as the MP and political reformist John Hampden who on 30 December 1685 pleaded guilty to treason and received the death sentence, but instead was fined a hefty £6,000.[33] The rebellion spawned a mixed crop of urban myths and conspiracy theories, most of them based on the premise that Monmouth had escaped and soon would be returning to settle old scores. Conversely there were demonstrations of loyalty to the king throughout the country, in places as far apart as London and Newcastle.[34] As he considered the post-rebellion scene James could feel some sense of satisfaction that he had successfully weathered the storm.

And yet, one nagging doubt persisted. How deeply were his daughter and son-in-law in the Netherlands involved in Monmouth's rebellion? When the trouble first began they had expressed their support for the king, and at James' request William had returned to England six regiments of foot (three English, three Scottish) which were based in the Netherlands on semi-loan under the terms of an agreement dating back in essence to the late sixteenth century. This Anglo-Dutch Brigade, as it was known, was made up mainly of English, Scottish and some Irish soldiers who were officially attached to the Dutch army, but could – as in this instance – be recalled to the service of the English monarch in times of crisis. Their loyalty to James was found to be dubious; they were not sent to deal with Monmouth but were kept in reserve at Hounslow and sent back to the Netherlands as soon as the crisis was over.[35]

On the other hand both William and Mary had certainly shown unwelcome partiality to Monmouth when he first arrived on their doorstep after the discovery of the Rye House plot. True, Mary was James' recognised heir, but nagging doubts nevertheless persisted.[36] Gradually, as his suspicions grew, he increasingly distanced himself from William (whom he was now actively beginning to dislike) and Mary, writing less frequently and pleading various demands on his time. His letters dealt not with affairs of state but with more mundane matters, especially the weather. Here is a typically banal sample:

> [18 November 1687: the king to the Prince of Orange] I have had yours
> ... by which I find you are come back to The Hague and that you have
> had as bad weather as we here. 'Twas high time to leave the country but
> the rains have not hindered me from fox hunting, nor the frost, which
> begun on Wednesday, from hunting that day. It has frozen ever since and [I]
> am afraid it will hinder me that sport on Monday next, it being likely to
> continue. I believe you have the same weather where you are. 'Tis late and
> I have not time to say more.[37]

This is hardly the stuff of which international diplomacy is made. Monmouth might have gone, but his disruptive influence remained.

4

TURBULENT TIMES

O n 6 September 1685 Francis North, Lord Guilford, styled Lord
Keeper of the Great Seal, died at his Oxfordshire country
seat of Wroxton. Two days later his brothers and joint executors, Dudley and Roger North, arrived in some state at Windsor, where
James II was currently resident, in order to hand over to him the symbol
of their late brother's office, the Great Seal itself. Roger later reported
that 'The King, who was in council, seemed surprised at the death of the
Lord Keeper, and took the Seal and dismissed us.' In another account of
the same incident he adds that the Seal was delivered 'in the bag (sealed)
into the King's own hand, who took the bag and asked if there was never
a purse (of state), and it was answered that none was brought down.
The King said no more to them, whereupon the executors retired.'[1] On
28 September the Seal was passed on to George Jeffreys, who stopped
off at Windsor to receive it on his way back to London from the blood-
letting in the West Country. The title then reverted to the more usual one
of Lord Chancellor.

Two features of this incident stand out. First, the naturally insensitive
side to James' nature is revealed in his enquiry about the missing state
purse in which the Great Seal was normally kept. The purse was a ceremonial bag heavily embroidered in gold and silver thread and with large
red tassels at the corners; it appears in the portrait of Lord Guilford in
the National Portrait Gallery and was an object of some value, so the
king's concern about it was perhaps not entirely misplaced. It is not clear
whether the purse had been left behind in London when Lord Guilford

made his final journey to Wroxton, or whether the North brothers had simply forgotten to bring it with them to Windsor. But it could be said that James was tactless to raise the question with them so bluntly at such a difficult time.

However, his attitude here is also closely linked to the second of these two points, namely his apparent failure to express to Dudley and Roger any kind of sympathy or regret on the loss of their elder brother. It seems they left his presence almost in disgrace, unwelcome and unregarded. Here is a further instance of James' inability to forgive and forget, for in fact he seems to have been projecting onto the unfortunate North brothers the animosity he had come to feel towards Lord Guilford and which had been so carefully nurtured by Jeffreys and Lord Sunderland. The days were long gone since Francis North's appointment as Lord Keeper in December 1682. At that time James, as Duke of York, had written in a letter to William of Orange that the death of the incumbent Lord Chancellor (Lord Nottingham) was imminent, and commenting that, 'It is believed that Lord Chief Justice North will succeed him, who is both able and bold, as well as loyal.'[2]

It is probable that the king's change in attitude towards Lord Guilford was triggered by the outcome of a case which came before his Lordship in 1684. In 1662 Alexander Fitton, a Catholic, had lost a lawsuit about property inheritance which he had brought against the distinguished Royalist soldier Lord Gerard of Brandon (later Earl of Macclesfield); moreover he had been imprisoned in 1663 for publishing a libellous pamphlet connected with the case and specifically with Brandon, and was not released until 1684. On the accession of King James, Fitton sensed that a new climate of opinion might work in his favour, and he applied to have the original conviction overturned. A re-hearing was arranged, and the king himself had a word in the ear of the Lord Keeper.[3]

He need not have bothered. Francis North listened to the case without comment, then finally, with the impartiality for which he was noted and which failed him only rarely, pronounced that the length of time that had elapsed since the original hearing was too long for the judgement to be changed, and that it must stand. From that time onwards, as his brother Roger was later to recall, 'the Roman Catholic party took umbrage from this judicial sentence, among other actions of his Lordship, to conclude he was inflexible to any purposes of theirs.'[4] No doubt James felt especially aggrieved, since he had taken a personal interest in the case. (Fitton was later knighted and made Lord Chancellor of Ireland; Lord Macclesfield, accused of complicity in the Rye House plot, fled to the Netherlands and joined other Whig notables in exile at the court of William and Mary.) However, the king was soon to feel even more annoyed with the disappointingly even-handed Lord Keeper.

The idea of a standing army was foreign to English tradition; over the centuries armies had been raised and disbanded as different situations demanded. The nearest thing to a more permanent arrangement had been the New Model Army raised by Cromwell, whose politics and military tactics both demanded a level of soldiering which a less well-drilled and cohesive body could never have reached. Inevitably the end of the Commonwealth brought with it a renewed aversion to anything like a professional army, so that any political moves towards setting one up were bound to be regarded by Parliament and the public alike with the utmost suspicion and apprehension. The bloodshed of the 1640s was still a painful memory, as was also the use of troops by unscrupulous rulers to impose their own rule on a reluctant population.

Back in 1667 Pepys had recorded MPs' disquiet at rumours that Charles II intended to retain the troops mustered at the time of the Dutch wars. 'Mr. Moore ... tells me he hears that the discontented Parliament-men are fearful that [at] the next sitting the King will put [in] for a general Excize, by which to raise him money, and then to fling off the Parliament, and raise a land-army and keep them all down like slaves' (7 July). On 25 July the MP Sir Thomas Tomkins rose to warn the House that 'all the country is grieved at this new-raised standing army'. The rumours were so strong that the king himself was at pains to refute them in his speech to Parliament on 29 July, as Pepys again reported: 'He did wonder that any should offer to bring in a suspicion that he intended to rule by an army or otherwise than by the laws of the land, which he promised them he would not.' The MPs were not persuaded, most continuing in the belief that the king and the Duke of York 'do what they can to get up an army, that they may need no more Parliaments'. (Another piece of gossip going the rounds and again relayed by Pepys related that Barbara Palmer herself had told Charles in no uncertain terms 'that he must rule by an Army or all would be lost'.) To keep a brake on the situation MPs more than once used the only effective weapon available to them, which was to deny the king the full supply of money which he said was needed to pay for the troops.

As a result of these tactics Charles was never able to build up an army of a size that he would have liked. After each of the three Dutch wars he was careful to disband the troops which had been specially raised for the emergency by a mixture of regular recruitment and forcible impress; indeed, given the attitude of Parliament, he had little choice in the matter. Nevertheless he did already have the nucleus of a regular standing army, formed principally by the two Guards regiments, the Coldstreams and the Grenadiers, and by the cavalry of the Life Guards and the Royal Horse Guards (later to be called the Blues).

The Coldstream Guards were first formed near the border town of Berwick-upon-Tweed in 1650 under the then Colonel George Monck, and were known as Monck's Regiment of Foot. They were crucial to Monck's control over Scotland during the years of the Commonwealth. On 1 January 1660 Monck led them out of the Northumbrian town of Coldstream (from which they soon took their name) on the long march down to London, where their discipline and authority helped to keep the peace during the sometimes bumpy transition to the Restoration. They proved to be so valuable in this role that they escaped the disband-ment visited on the rest of the New Model Army and were officially recognised as permanent guardians of the monarch.

The Grenadier Guards began life in Bruges as the bodyguard of the exiled Charles II, with the title of the Royal Regiment of Guards, and returned with him to England in 1660, where a second Regiment was formed. In 1665 both Regiments were amalgamated into a single unit of twenty-four Companies as the First Regiment of Foot Guards. A 17-year-old junior officer who joined as an Ensign in 1667 was John Churchill.[5] The two cavalry regiments were similarly founded in the pre-Restoration period as bodyguards, originally composed of loyal and enthusiastic gentlemen, and in 1661 they were officially established with the obligation to attend upon the persons of the king and the Duke of York as required.

It seems clear that King James was determined to outdo his brother by building up a large standing army in order to reinforce his authority, though how far he would actually have gone in using it to suppress opposition is an open question. Some had no doubts at all about his intentions. 'It seems to me that the King of England is very glad to have a pretence for raising troops and he believes that the Duke of Monmouth's enterprise will serve only to make him still more master of his country.' So wrote the French Ambassador, Paul Barillon, to his master Louis XIV.[6] In earlier years James had certainly nurtured thoughts if not hopes of absolute rule, free from the shackles of Parliament and backed up by military force. If this was indeed his intention, the rebellion had now given him the perfect excuse. At the time of his accession in February 1685 the army in England consisted of almost 9,000 men – a laughably small number by contemporary Continental standards. By the end of the Monmouth rebellion in July of the same year the total had shot up to well over 15,000 and by the end of the year had further risen to almost 20,000.[7] Alarmingly, James made no move to reduce these numbers, but instead justified them on the grounds that the rebellion had shown the need to keep sufficient troops under arms to resist any threat to Crown or country.

It had also highlighted another problem – the alleged unreliability of the militia or trained bands. In James' view these part-time soldiers, mostly organised on county lines, had shown themselves to be an ill-equipped and poorly-trained force, totally unable to engage Monmouth's forces in battle. He ignored the fact that they had been of considerable use in disrupting Monmouth's lines of communication and distracting the rebels with unexpected skirmishes and sallies. He saw only an untrustworthy bunch of amateurs who could not be relied upon in any future crisis and whose place would be far better filled by expanded numbers of regular soldiery. This was a situation which he was determined to resolve.

The king was therefore not pleased to find himself taken to task over this and other matters by the Lord Keeper. Some time in late July or early August, Francis North had made the most of the opportunity of a private audience to raise his deep concerns over the way things in general seemed to be going, and with some courage had pointed out the various pitfalls that might lie ahead. 'As to his army, his Lordship said that upon a universal discontent he [James] would find it a broken reed.' He also warned the king not to alienate the nation by unpopular policies, reminding him (perhaps rather tactlessly) that 'Although the Duke of Monmouth was gone, yet there was a P[rince] of O[range] on the other side of the water'.[8] Allegiances, hinted North, could change all too quickly and easily if people were pushed too far. Already out of favour, his advice was not well received. And so, tired, depressed and seriously unwell, he was readily given permission to retire to Wroxton where he died a few weeks later.

Impervious to criticism, it was in a new mood of self-confidence and assertiveness that James now summoned Parliament to reconvene on 9 November 1685, delivering a long and uncompromising speech from the throne. Unsurprisingly using the recent rebellion as a prime example, he stressed the need to maintain a sizeable body of troops under arms and asked MPs to vote enough money for its upkeep. 'Nothing,' he told them, 'but a good force of well-disciplined troops in constant pay ... can defend us from such as either at home or abroad are disposed to disturb us.' He further declared that the essential corollary to this was reform of the militia, even to its abolition and replacement by regular troops.

His words threw the House of Commons into a state of agitation and an anxious debate ensued, in which opposition to the idea of a standing army was freely and widely expressed. So far as the militia were concerned, the House was reluctant to see them permanently disbanded and instead suggested reform, to be enshrined in a Bill. Providing funds for the proposed army was another vexed question. Various sums were suggested, but in the end a figure of £700,000 was agreed, although the Members declined to state that the money was to be spent specifically on the army.

But the king's speech contained an even more contentious issue. Although it seems that the matter had already been discussed in cabinet, James now for the first time publicly admitted the presence in the army of a number of Roman Catholic officers. Under the terms of the Test Act these officers were legally disqualified to serve, and their continued presence was another cause of great disquiet, so strong was the latent fear of Catholicism. Their recruitment during the Monmouth uprising had been presented as a necessary but temporary arrangement (there were, it was said, not enough trained Protestant officers available at short notice), but now James defiantly announced that he intended to keep them in post. 'I will neither expose them to disgrace, nor myself to the want of them, if there should be another Rebellion to make them necessary to me,' he stated bluntly.

However well disposed the House of Commons may have been initially towards the new monarch, this was too much. After serious debate, backed up by some plain speaking in the Lords, the House sent its response to the king, reminding him politely but firmly that 'those officers cannot by law be capable of their employments, and that the incapacities they bring upon themselves thereby, can in no way be taken off but by an act of Parliament'.[9]

James was furious. He sent word that he 'did not expect such an address from the House of Commons', and on 20 November ordered that Parliament should be prorogued, a process which was to be repeated at intervals until the final dissolution on 2 July 1687. After that date Parliament did not meet again during the reign of James II.

In dismissing the Members so abruptly James had deprived himself of the funds which, though agreed, had not been finally approved. In truth he did not need the money. The funds which Parliament had voted him at his accession, plus the increased revenues from the new taxes which had been imposed at the same time, meant that his newly enlarged army could be maintained for the foreseeable future without further reference to the Commons. This gave him a freedom of action which earlier monarchs might well have envied, and despite Parliament's misgivings the army remained under arms. Each year from 1685 until 1688 it assembled for several weeks of the summer months in an encampment on Hounslow Heath, then an area of scrubland several miles from London. Here it drilled and trained in battle conditions, giving families from London the chance of a really good day out, much as people today go to watch historical re-enactments of the Civil War or other conflicts.[10] The king himself, keen to bring his new army up to the standards of its various Continental counterparts, was often present in a supervisory role. The royal tents were provided with full dining facilities, and there was even a temporary chapel.[11]

When not at Hounslow the soldiers dispersed countrywide to the various garrison towns where they were stationed, though not to barracks, for they had none. Instead they were regularly billeted on an unwilling mixture of inns, taverns and private householders – a most unsatisfactory arrangement, the more so because a sadly high proportion of the troops were ill-disciplined, drunken, prone to theft and violence, and generally badly behaved. There were also frequent quarrels between Protestant officers and their Catholic counterparts, many of which ended in duelling and death. Amongst the Protestants it had come to be widely believed that eventually they would all be replaced by Catholics, and this did not make for cordial relations.[12] Speaking of his attitude towards a standing army, the poet Edmund Waller, who was also MP for Sandwich, said that he found himself to be 'more now against it than I lately was, being satisfied that the country is weary of the oppression of the soldiers, weary of free quarters, plunder, and some felons, for which they [i.e. the people] have no complaint, no redress'.[13]

Growing ever more confident of his position, James now turned his attention towards finding a legal loophole for the official employment of the Catholic army officers – a ruse which he hoped would also enable him to introduce Catholics into public office under the umbrella of general religious toleration, towards which he was genuinely sympathetic. He had begun to set much store on a single word – dispensation. A modern dictionary definition of this word is 'Licence or permission to neglect a rule; ground of exemption', and James' interpretation of it had already been made clear through his mouthpiece Jeffreys. At his first appearance on the woolsack as Lord Chancellor at the opening of Parliament on 9 November, the complaisant Jeffreys had strongly endorsed 'the legality and expediency of the power of the Sovereign to dispense with laws for the safety and benefit of the State'.[14] His speech, raising as it did the spectre of autocratic rule, was ill-received, and did nothing to make the king's own speech, which followed, any more palatable. The concept and indeed use of royal dispensing powers post-1661 was not entirely novel, but it had been sparingly and carefully used by Charles II so as to avoid public condemnation. Now that it had been brought out into the open, its dangers had been all too plainly revealed. It was now obvious to James and his ministers that a more subtle approach would be needed.

Accordingly Jeffreys was instructed to approach the chief legal figures in the land and to seek their personal opinions in writing as to the legality of the royal dispensing powers. As the queen's Attorney-General, Roger North gave a reply in which his carefully judged language could not conceal his profound belief that such powers were not legal, and this indeed was the reaction of all his colleagues. Roger, always the soul of honesty, was under no illusions. 'If I had been pert and forward, as in truth I was perfectly otherwise, as being modest and diffident, I might have gone into the closet and told what [good] opinion I had of the king's dispensing power, and have laid up a sure interest for preferment.'[15] Instead he spoke the truth and this, as in the case of his brother Francis, immediately marked him out as a potential obstacle to the king's intentions.

Roger soon had another cause for concern. In June 1686 the case of *Godden v. Hales* came before a panel of twelve judges sitting in the court of King's Bench, the presiding judge being the current Lord Chief Justice, Sir Edward Herbert. Such an impressive array of legal minds had clearly been assembled for a purpose which at first sight the case itself hardly seemed to merit – indeed, if anything, it all appeared slightly ludicrous. Sir Edward Hales, a Catholic convert, was indicted by his coachman, Arthur Godden, on the grounds that, as an aspiring army colonel, he had failed to take the oaths imposed by the Test Act. Hardly an earth-shaking cause, it might be thought. Yet there was much more to the case than met the eye. The statutory penalty for the offence was a fine of £500, and where a prosecution was brought by an individual, that person was entitled to claim the fine for himself. It could therefore be said that Godden had brought the accusation with the primary aim of raising money for his own pocket. However, the weight of legal opinion brought to bear on the case shows that this would be too naïve a conclusion.

In fact the case was a set-up, designed to bring in a verdict which would put the stamp of legality on the king's dispensing powers. Before the hearing James himself had selected the judges, making sure that they – unlike the individuals who had been previously canvassed by Jeffreys – would produce the result he wanted. Six of the judges originally chosen had shown signs of resisting his wishes, so they had been replaced by more compliant colleagues.[16] After counsel had set out their arguments and the bench had conferred, the Lord Chief Justice duly delivered the collective judgement which, with one courageous dissention, unsurprisingly asserted that the sovereign, as the fountain-head of all law, was empowered as of right to override the law when circumstances demanded. On this basis Sir Edward's appointment was confirmed. The verdict, with its strong whiff of corruption, was widely unpopular, but it was enough to satisfy James and to hand him the legal weapon for which he had sought. He lost no time in using it.

One of James' first acts under this new legal umbrella was to appoint five Catholic peers and a Jesuit priest, Edward Petre, to his Privy Council.[17] He had been encouraged to take this step by his principal Secretary of State, Robert Spencer, 2nd Earl of Sunderland. The Earl had risen in politics under Charles II to become a Secretary of State and Ambassador to Paris, but in 1681 had opposed the succession of the then Duke of York and had openly sided with the Exclusionists, for which he had been dismissed. Having then managed to convince Charles (mainly, it is said, through the intercession of Barbara Palmer) that it had all been a terrible misunderstanding, he was re-appointed to various consecutive posts including those of Secretary of State and Lord President of the Council, and it was as Secretary of State that he was officiating when King Charles died. Perhaps conscious of his 1681 *faux-pas* and aware that his new master had a long memory for grievances, he immediately took zealous action to ensure a smooth transition of power, such as closing ports and introducing press censorship, and was rewarded with unconditional reinstatement in his post.[18]

From then on Lord Sunderland lost no opportunity to prove his loyalty to the Crown and his readiness to support James at every turn, and indeed in 1688, on the very eve of the Revolution, he went so far as to convert to Catholicism himself. This was an act which, however sincere at the time, must now inevitably be seen as one of cynical opportunism, especially when it was followed by his reconversion to Anglicanism once the Revolution had been established. Today Lord Sunderland would be described as unprincipled, a smooth operator, a fixer *par excellence*, although in fact he was no better or worse than most politicians of his time – only that much more cunning and astute than they were. Three hundred and more years later he is brought suddenly to life for us by Roger North, who had a good ear for vocal inflexions and who introduces us to an affected manner of speech that was apparently promoted at court by Sunderland during the post-Restoration years. The Earl 'in speaking had made it almost a fashion to distend the vocal letters' (i.e. to prolong the vowels) and in so doing produced what Roger calls his 'court tune'. Sunderland's ridiculous drawl is preserved in the following passage taken verbatim from a speech in the House of Lords which the Earl made during the reign of Charles II: 'Whaat, if his Maajesty tarn out faarty of us, may not he have faarty athers [forty others] to saarve him as well? And whaat maaters who saarves his Maajesty, so lang as his Maajesty is saarved?' ('Such reasoning *saarved* for want of better', was Roger's acid comment.)[19]

Something of this seems to have rubbed off onto Titus Oates. On attending a House of Commons inquiry as an onlooker and not liking the inconclusive outcome of the proceedings, he shouted out 'Aw Laard, aw Laard, aw, aw!' and barged out of the room in a fury.[20]

If the king and his lackey Sunderland had hoped that the Anglican Church would not notice the creeping tide of Catholicism lapping around it, they were to be disappointed. Their methods, after all, were hardly subtle. Catholic worship was now openly encouraged, and a number of Catholic chapels appeared in the larger towns such as Worcester and Bristol, while in London by late 1688 there were eighteen such chapels.[21]

The establishment of these chapels sometimes provoked public disturbances of varying intensity. Whilst keen not to antagonise the Anglicans,
James nevertheless made sure that bishoprics, as they became vacant, were
filled by nominees who were *ipso facto* sympathetic towards his policies.
Thus in late 1686 the important sees of Oxford and Chester were allotted
to Samuel Parker and Thomas Cartwright respectively, both churchmen
known for their supportive attitude towards the king. He soon had cause
to welcome it.

In March 1686 James had reissued a directive to the Anglican Church,
entitled *Directions to Preachers*. First produced under Charles II in 1662,
it ordered that sermons and pastoral teaching were specifically to avoid
religious controversy and to keep strictly to ethical and moral themes.[22]
Many anti-Catholic clergy resented this attempt to stifle their perceived
duty, which was to warn their congregations against the perils of popery.
Some no doubt quietly rebelled, but were not taken to task. However,
one example in particular was sufficiently public to attract official attention and to provoke action. In May Dr John Sharp, rector of the London
church of St Giles-in-the-Fields (and who in the pluralistic climate of
the times was also Dean of Norwich), delivered a sermon 'in which he
zealously reproov'd the Doctrine of the R[oman] C[hurch]', reported
Evelyn on 8 September. When news of this attack reached the ears of
James he was understandably enraged. As a result, Henry Compton, who
as Bishop of London since 1675 was in today's terms John Sharp's line-
manager, received royal instructions to suspend the disobedient cleric
from duty. In his letter to the bishop, written from Windsor on 14 June
1686, James complained that Dr Sharp had 'presumed to make unbecoming Reflections, and to utter such Expressions as were not fit or proper
for him: and endeavouring thereby to beget in the Minds of his Hearers
an Evil Opinion of Us and our Government ... and to lead them into
Disobedience and Rebellion'.[23]

But the bishop did not suspend Dr Sharp. Instead he wrote to
Lord Sunderland as Lord President of the Council, declaring that, 'I
sent to Mr. Dean [i.e. Sharp] and acquainted him with His Majesty's
Displeasure,' assuring Sunderland that he had found Sharp 'ready to give
all Reasonable Satisfaction'. For good measure he made Sharp deliver the

letter in person to the court at Windsor.[24] Sharp also wrote to the king himself, apologising for his conduct. But the fact remained that he had not been suspended.

Bishop Compton was everything that, in the eyes of James, made him an ecclesiastical *persona non grata*. On his consecration as Bishop of Oxford in 1674, followed by his move to London in the following year, things had looked more promising; he was appointed to the Privy Council, and selected to oversee the education and spiritual welfare of the princesses Mary and Anne.[25] But the energy with which he charitably took up the cause of Non-conformity and tried to draw Dissenters back into the Anglican flock was equalled only by his implacable opposition to Catholicism in any shape or form. On the accession of James II the bishop was summarily dismissed from the Privy Council and also from his additional post as Dean of the Chapel Royal. Undaunted, he spoke out strongly in the House of Lords against the royal dispensing powers. His failure to discipline John Sharp was – or so it seemed to the exasperated James – a defiant and deliberate challenge to the royal authority which must not be allowed to pass unnoticed. Yet, however strong his feelings, the king could not bring himself to confront Compton personally. The bishop was, after all, a son of the Earl of Northampton, was robust and fearless, and was not without powerful friends. Nor could the Anglican Church itself, with its anti-Catholic bias, be expected to discipline him. Instead, James came up with a new idea.

This was for an Ecclesiastical Commission, which would oversee the functioning of the Church on behalf of the king, including the making of appointments and the exercise and maintenance of discipline. Its powers also stretched to the Universities, all the colleges of both Oxford and Cambridge being closely connected to the established Church. The Commission was no toothless animal; indeed the roll-call of its members reflected the importance with which James now invested it. The seven members included Lord Chancellor Jeffreys, Lord Sunderland, and the bishops of Durham and Rochester. The Archbishop of Canterbury (William Sancroft), though selected, refused to stand.

The Commission's first and most obvious task was to deal with Bishop Compton. Three separate hearings were held, on 4 and 9 August and

6 September. The bishop's defence was that there were no legal grounds on which he could have proceeded against Dr Sharp. He further suggested that the Commission itself was illegal and that he ought rather to be heard in an ecclesiastical court composed of his fellow bishops.[26] The Lord Chancellor was having none of this. Jeffreys behaved in his usual hectoring way, dominating the proceedings and (as Evelyn tells us) ensuring that 'the Bishop was sentenc'd, without so much as being heard to any purpose: which was thought a very extraordinary way of proceeding, & [was] universally resented' (8 September 1686). The bishop's punishment was suspension at the king's pleasure from all his duties, the same penalty being applied to Dr Sharp. It was to be two years before Henry Compton was able to return to office on the tide of the impending Revolution, although John Sharp's unobtrusive reappearance took place rather sooner.

The final Compton hearing took place, as seen, in early September. In October James made his first significant move on the University front, with the appointment of the pro-Catholic John Massey as Dean of Christ Church. In the following January he ordered the appointment of Joshua Bassett as Master of Sidney Sussex College, Cambridge. Bassett was a convert to Catholicism, and his appointment ignored a provision in the Elizabethan statues of the College which required that any incoming Master was obliged to swear an oath against popery.[27] An appeal by the Fellows of the College to the Ecclesiastical Commission had no effect and Bassett was duly installed.

The king's biggest battle on this front was with Magdalen College, Oxford. Again there was a vacancy for the head or (at Magdalen) President of the College, following the death of the incumbent (Dr Clarke) in March 1687. Again James sought to fill it with his own pro-Catholic nominee, even though the legal right to make the appointment rested not with the Crown but with the Fellows of the College. His candidate, Anthony Farmer, was perhaps the most unsuitable that could have been found, for quite apart from the Catholic sympathies for which he had been selected he was a habitual drunkard and was known for lewd and lecherous behaviour, although in fairness it must be said that at the time James probably had no knowledge of this. The Fellows were appalled. Surely, they reasoned, the king had been badly briefed on the situation? As time was short and there was a deadline, they decided to proceed according to the College statutes, and on 15 April they elected one of their number, Dr John Hough – a staunch Anglican – to the Presidency of the College.

Yet again James was enraged. In June the Ecclesiastical Commission was convened to deal with the case, but the Fellows of Magdalen were not overawed and doggedly maintained their stance that they alone had the right to nominate their President. However, they had reckoned without the king's newly confirmed dispensing powers. The Commission declared Hough's appointment to be null and void and the king then imposed on the College his next choice as its President, the compliant Bishop of Oxford (Samuel Parker), despite the fact that the bishop had himself confirmed Hough's appointment. Still the Fellows resisted; even a personal visit from James in September and a royal tongue-lashing ('Is this your Church of England's loyalty? ... I will be obeyed!' he shouted) made no difference to their adamant refusal to recognise his candidate or to abandon their sworn duty towards the College.[28] Parker's 'election' stood, but for James it was something of a Pyrrhic victory. Ignored by the Fellows – who were in any case ejected by the Commission – Parker duly admitted Catholics to the College (including some Jesuits), but he was already a sick man at the time of his disputed installation on 25 October and died five months later on 21 March 1688.

SCIENCE MAKES THE GRADE

The Royal Society is a world-respected forum for many of today's finest scientific minds. Except for the greatly increased range of its influence it has not changed significantly since its beginnings. These were in the 1640s and '50s, when small groups of men interested in mathematics, philosophy, scientific experiments, astronomy and related subjects began to hold meetings in Oxford and London, perhaps spurred on by similar developments in France. After 1660 these meetings were held on a regular basis and were concentrated in London at Gresham College, a foundation (which still exists) established in 1596 for the provision of regular public lectures on topics such as law, theology, astronomy and music. Amongst the earliest supporters of the meetings were some of the most brilliant scientifically minded figures of the age, including Christopher Wren (already a celebrated astronomer and mathematician before he took to architecture), the scientist Robert Hooke, the chemist Robert Boyle and the mathematician John Wallis. Others whose interests, though more general, were no less strong included John Evelyn and, later, Samuel Pepys (elected 1665, President 1684–86).

The group, as reconstituted after the Restoration, met for the first time in November 1660 and consisted of twelve members. It was not to remain so small for much longer. At the same meeting it was decided to invite forty more selected members to join, most of whom accepted and were duly elected. The majority were not specialists but, like Evelyn and Pepys, had enquiring minds which, in the spirit of the times, thirsted for any kind of scientific knowledge. The November meeting also agreed to seek royal patronage which, it was hoped, would set the seal of approval on a body that might otherwise face some public opposition. After all, the notion of science, in any shape or form, was still a problem to a generation not yet entirely freed from the shackles of medieval superstitions and religious taboos.

Accordingly King Charles was approached and on 15 July 1662 gave his royal seal of approval to a charter. This gave the group the desired respectability, as well as certain privileges including the macabre right to carry out human dissections, and a name – the Royal Society. In the following year the name was resoundingly upgraded to the Royal Society of London for the Promotion of Natural Knowledge. The members now became Fellows, one of whom was James, Duke of York. Both the duke and his royal brother took a keen interest in the proceedings of the Society and attended its meetings. The king in particular was fascinated by a wide variety of scientific topics and had a laboratory set up in Whitehall, so that he could carry out his own experiments. He was especially interested in the properties of mercury – an interest which is thought by some to have contributed to his death. On 15 January 1669 Pepys was taken 'into the King's little elaboratory[sic] … and there saw a great many Chymicall glasses and things, but understood none of them'.

As a mark of approval Charles presented the Society with a silver mace. However it seems that in private he did not always treat the Society with due respect. 'Gresham College he mightily laughed at for spending time only in weighing of ayre, and doing nothing else since they sat,' reported Pepys on 1 February 1664. Gresham College was the actual meeting place, but Pepys – and others – also used it as a synonym for the Society.

There was of course much more to the Society's various experiments than the king's derisive comment would suggest; in fact they formed a highly significant part of its activities. In 1662 Robert Hooke was appointed Curator of Experiments (from 1677 to 1682 he was the Society's Secretary). Hooke was something of an enigmatic figure, whose prickly and irascible *persona* concealed a scintillating intelligence. The barometer, quadrant, thermometer, balance spring and telescope were all studied and developed by him. In the field of architecture he provided several designs for buildings in London, such as the original Bethlehem Hospital (Bedlam), and he assisted Wren in making the official survey of London after the Great Fire of 1666, as well as helping to design some of the new City churches. His pioneering use of the microscope led to his most celebrated publication *Micrographia* (1665), in which such things as the eye of a fly or the transparent body of a flea are exquisitely engraved in close-up detail. Pepys bought a copy hot off the press and was delighted with it: 'To my booksellers and [from] there took home Hookes book of Microscopy, a most excellent piece, and of which I am very proud' (20 January 1665).

As Curator, Hooke presided over a variety of experiments, some useful, some less obviously so (such as converting a piece of roast mutton into blood, or depriving a kitten of air by means of a suction pump), and gave lectures himself on a broad choice of subjects ranging from astronomy to felt-making. The wide diversity of the Society's interests ensured that a good proportion of its findings were beneficial. In addition, its official status meant that it could act as a clearing-house for the exchange of scientific ideas without fear of persecution or enforced closure – a bonus point which attracted a number of foreign correspondents.

The later years of the seventeenth century saw the Society grow in prestige and influence both at home and abroad. Part of this was due to the glory reflected from the more eminent members, two of whom in particular (apart from Hooke) stood out from their colleagues. The name of Robert Boyle, who is sometimes called 'the father of modern chemistry', is widely known today through 'Boyle's Law', which deals with the proportionable balance between the pressure and volume of gases. However, this in itself gives little indication of the range of Boyle's research and experiments, many of which he carried out in the house which he shared with his sister in Pall Mall. There were few scientific topics and theories which he did not investigate, and he also looked forward into the future, suggesting such miracles as the possibility of flight.

Even Boyle's gifts were overshadowed by the towering genius of Isaac Newton, who joined the Royal Society in 1672 and became its President in 1703. During these years he perfected some of his most momentous discoveries, including those on optics and gravitation, and published his seminal works *De Motu Corporum in Gyrum* (1684) and *Philosophiæ Naturalis Principia Mathematica* (1687). Yet his was no ivory tower, and as Master of Trinity (his old Cambridge college) from 1683, he vehemently objected to King James' attempts to interfere with the University constitution. On the strength of these objections he was elected to serve as an MP representing his University in the Convention Parliament of 1689. Not even England's greatest scientific mind could ignore the impact of the Glorious Revolution.

It may seem strange that despite his strong Catholic faith and consequent surrounding of himself with a proportion of Catholic advisors and
supporters, James was basically in favour of religious toleration – more
so, in fact, than the hierarchy of the Anglican Church. This appears to
conflict with the popularly held perception of him, both today and in
his own time, as a religious fanatic intent on immediately reimposing
Catholicism as the official religion of the country. In fact James' views
on the ultimate supremacy of Catholicism had not changed, but he was
enough of a realist to recognise that it could not be achieved directly
without an unacceptable level of violence and bloodshed. On the other
hand toleration, whilst in itself ethically desirable, would also make it that
much easier to admit Catholics to public office, and so ultimately not
only change the balance of religious influence but also alter and dominate the entire social and political landscape.

Thus in James' philosophy, while Dissenters of most Non-conformist
persuasions were undoubtedly a means to an end, they nevertheless
should be allowed to worship in their own way, provided they kept a
low profile and did not try to make political waves. However, there was a
formidable obstacle to this goal in the shape of the Test Act. This was too
big a problem to be dealt with under the royal dispensing powers. The
Act would have to be repealed in Parliament, but it was not at all certain
that Parliament would be in favour of this, or even that there would be a
national appetite for such a change.

One interim solution offered itself, and James took it. On 4 April 1687
he published a *Declaration to all his loving subjects for Liberty of Conscience*,
also known as the Declaration of Indulgence, which suspended (but did
not, could not permanently abolish) the penal laws previously applied
to all Dissenters and Non-conformists in England and Wales. To these
groups he now formally announced that 'we do freely give them leave
to meet and serve God after their own way and manner, be it in private
houses, or places … hired or built for that use,' so long as their meetings were peaceful, public and politically non-controversial.[29] As a means
of testing the waters, he had already published a similar Declaration in
Scotland back in February, and the fact that on the whole it had gone
down well there emboldened him to produce the English version.

Scotland proved a useful testing-ground for James' theories of toleration. In February 1686, exactly a year earlier than the Scottish version of the Declaration, he had issued an order that in Scotland not only Catholics but also Quakers – a previously much-persecuted group – were to be allowed freedom to worship at home. A few months later most of the Quakers languishing in English gaols (over 1,000) were released. Significantly, James selected the prominent Quaker William Penn as his emissary to the Netherlands, with the task of persuading William and Mary that it would be right and proper to repeal the Test Act. Penn failed, though he remained useful to James as a go-between with access to the main Non-conformist elements in the country.

He failed because, to James' annoyance, William and Mary (advised by Gilbert Burnet – see Chapter 5) declared themselves to be adamantly opposed to any repeal of the Test Act. Early in 1687 James also tried to make his point to the Dutch emissary Everaard van Dijkvelt (Dijkveldt) but, following William's instructions, Dijkvelt was more interested in giving secret assurances of William's support to the anti-James faction. What really scared William and Mary was the possibility that James' brand of tolerance would ease so many Catholics and their supporters into positions of power and influence that there would be renewed unrest and even civil war in England. The resultant chaos could, they felt, encourage Louis XIV to restart his military adventures against the Netherlands.

Throughout the months of 1686 and '87 James had also been taking soundings individually from prominent officials and MPs on their attitude towards the final repeal of the Test Act. The method of interrogation was called 'closeting' and involved a private and personal interview with the king himself. Amongst those summoned were Roger North, still the queen's Attorney-General, and his brother Dudley. Dudley's response to the king's yes-or-no demand for support was 'that he could not, and therefore would not, pretend to tell what he should do upon any question proposed in Parliament … till he heard the debate'. Roger, confronted by a formidable duo of James plus Lord Chancellor Jeffreys, also proved to be a disappointment. Asked if he would vote on the king's side in Parliament, he replied that, if he were to give his promise to do so, and then found his opinion being swayed by Parliamentary debate, 'it would make me mad'. In other words, he could not in all honesty give any such promise. James then quoted Scripture, 'He that is not for us is against us,' adding that, 'I hope I shall not find you so, for it will be very inconvenient.' Roger's response to this was, that if he were to die in the next moment, he could not say otherwise. 'Why then, in plain English, you are a trimmer,' said James crossly, and abruptly dismissed him from the royal presence. Today's plain English would probably replace 'trimmer' with 'fence-sitter'.

To do him justice, 'The King showed no [further] tokens of his displeasure, nor did he in any case when the persons appeared respectful and he thought them sincere,' wrote Roger. But he also noted that there was a change in the social temperature at court: 'The times began to grow sour, all favour leaned towards the Catholics and such as prostituted to that interest.'[30] Loyal to the Crown yet also to the established Anglican Church, Roger North typified those public servants whose divided loyalties forced them to withdraw from office and seek early retirement, rather than become embroiled in the politics of the day.

Angered by the refusal of William and Mary to entertain any thoughts of repealing the Test Act, and painfully aware that his own efforts to gain support for his policies were getting nowhere, James abruptly dissolved Parliament on 2 July 1687.[31] It had become clear to him that the only way of getting the Test Act repealed would be to hold elections for a new Parliament and to make sure that it was packed with enough Whig sympathisers to ensure a majority for the repeal. On the king's behalf Lord Sunderland at once began work to secure the necessary votes. All those public office holders who would have a hand in the selection of Parliamentary candidates or who might themselves qualify for selection as MPs would have to be carefully chosen. Unfortunately many of those already in post were pro-Anglican, anti-repeal Tories. They would have to go. Wholesale sackings followed; lord lieutenants, sheriffs, JPs, civic corporations, the City of London livery guilds, militia officers – none were safe from the predatory incursions of James. Yet for the most part their replacements were hardly satisfactory. While those Dissenters propelled into public office welcomed their new religious freedom, most of them had no wish to be members of a Parliament which they rightly suspected would be used to push Catholics into positions of power. In the civic communities, many of the new Whig town councillors were inexperienced nobodies who lacked any enthusiasm for their work, and who did little or nothing to promote the king's cause at local level, as was expected of them.

The need to raise local awareness of the important issues at stake prompted James to undertake a tour or progress through a number of English towns and cities, from 16 August until 6 September. The list of the principal places he visited in the space of these three weeks makes impressive reading, especially bearing in mind the state of the roads at that period – deeply rutted, sticky with mud in winter, covered with powdery, easily-disturbed dust in summer. Moreover, even the most luxurious coaches with their padded upholstery had no springs; instead, they were slung from broad leather straps and swayed about with a motion that must have brought on many a case of travel sickness. Toughened by his military and naval experiences, James is unlikely to have succumbed to any such weakness. He stopped off at Portsmouth, Bath, Gloucester, Worcester, Ludlow, Shrewsbury, Whitchurch, Chester, Newport, Lichfield, Coventry, Banbury, Oxford and Cirencester, before returning to Bath and so back to Windsor.[32] At Oxford on 4 September there took place the painful interview with the Fellows of Magdalen College. Wherever his cavalcade stopped, James took the opportunity to lecture the townspeople, town councils and individual hosts on the virtues of tolerance and the need to repeal the Test Act.

For the most part he was received politely, even – in some places – with apparent enthusiasm, and listened to respectfully, but there was no way of telling whether his message was really getting through. (It was reported to William of Orange that 'in all the King's progress very few of the gentry waited on his Majesty'.)[33] And so it was with some exasperation, if not desperation, that in the spring of 1688 James and his advisors, led by Lord Sunderland, decided that the time had come to raise the profile of the Declaration of Indulgence countrywide and to give it a more public airing. In choosing the pulpits of the Anglican Church as his platform from which to deliver the message, the king made his most serious mistake so far.

DUTCH COURAGE – NEW HOPE

O n 4 May 1688 King James issued a royal edict requiring that all Anglican bishops must direct their clergy to read out the Declaration of Indulgence to their congregations. The reading was ordered to take place on consecutive Sundays, 20 and 27 May in London, and 3 and 10 June in the rest of the country. Deeply troubled and alarmed by this development, the Archbishop of Canterbury summoned a synod of bishops and other leading churchmen at Lambeth Palace on 12 May to discuss the situation.

William Sancroft (b. 1617) had been Dean successively of York Minster and St Paul's Cathedral. In 1668 he was appointed Archdeacon of Canterbury and was consecrated Archbishop ten years later. A man of integrity, humility and steadfast faith, he worked hard to augment unacceptably low clerical incomes and to endow newly created parishes in fast-growing urban areas, especially in the North of England. He founded and endowed a school at Harleston in Norfolk, and had intended to do the same for his Suffolk birthplace of Fressingfield, though this project came to nothing. Other similar schemes which were doubtless considered and in some instances may have been followed through were tantalisingly summarised by his steward Roger North as 'divers other matters of that kind'. The up-and-coming barrister North had been surprised to find himself appointed steward to the See of Canterbury in 1679 (probably through the influence of his brother Francis, the Lord Keeper) but soon developed a great admiration for the archbishop, whose close attention to detail never ceased to impress him deeply:

> It was to me a wonder to observe the industry of that man. If any presented him, as many did, with discourses upon business impending, he would register them in his own books with his own hand, using his exquisite orthography and abbreviations, and mending the English and periodising in all places, as ought to be done. And he did me the honour to do the like with all he received from me.[1]

Over the past months the archbishop had observed with mounting concern the increasingly threatening situation developing between the established Church and the Crown, and had recognised the conflict of loyalties which this involved. On the one hand, if the bishops and clergy refused to carry out the king's orders, their sworn loyalty to the Crown would be broken. On the other hand, to read out the Declaration would be to give tacit approval to a tolerance and indeed encouragement of Catholicism (and, to a lesser extent, Dissent) which up till then had been regularly and vigorously denounced from the majority of Anglican pulpits. This was precisely the kind of dilemma that had already caused Sancroft to withdraw from the Ecclesiastical Commission.

Prolonged and agonised discussion between the bishops took place over several days at Lambeth, but on 18 May it was agreed that a petition should be presented to the king, the clergy 'praying to be excused from reading or distributing his late Declaration'. It was stressed that this request arose not from any wish to be undutiful, but simply because the dispensing power, which had enabled James to make the Declaration, had been declared illegal by Parliament. Sancroft wrote out the petition in his own hand and signed it, together with six other bishops. Despite the lateness of the hour (10 p.m.) it was determined that the six bishops should take a boat to Whitehall and present the petition to the king in person. The archbishop himself decided to remain at Lambeth, due to a combination of the lateness of the hour, his age (71) and his poor health (he had a bad cough at the time).

The personality of the bishops is usually submerged in their collective group, so for the record they deserve to be identified as individuals in their own right. They were Thomas Ken (Bath and Wells), John Lake (Chichester), William Lloyd (St Asaph), the Cornish baronet Sir Jonathan Trelawny (Bristol), Francis Turner (Ely) and Thomas White (Peterborough). Of them all it is probably Thomas Ken who is the best remembered today, if only because he wrote the words of two hymns which are still sung; these are *Glory to Thee, my God, this night* and *Awake, my soul*. Devotees of angling may like to know that he was the brother-in-law of Izaak Walton, who thought highly of him and left him a mourning ring. Similarly, musicians will appreciate his reputation as a performer on the lute, viol and organ; he also had a good singing voice.

A conscientious parish priest, Thomas Ken progressed up the clerical ladder and was selected as a chaplain to Charles II. When Nell Gwynn (the self-confessed 'Protestant whore') sent word that she wanted to take over his house in Winchester during the king's summer visit to that city, she received, not fawning consent, but a stinging rebuke. Dr Ken sent a message whose kernel was 'that no woman living in open defiance of God's law should abide under the shadow of his roof'. That roof, he expected, would now fall in under the weight of the king's wrath. Nothing happened. On the contrary, when some time later the see of Bath and Wells became vacant, Charles is recorded as saying, 'Where is the good little man who refused the lodging to poor Nell? I intend the bishopric … for Dr. Ken, and it is my own especial appointment.' Ken was duly consecrated at Lambeth on 25 January 1685. When on the following 2 February the king was taken ill, it was Ken who, although the junior cleric present at his bedside, nevertheless took the lead in ministering to his spiritual needs and in trying to persuade him to receive the Sacrament. The new king James also had a high opinion of Bishop Ken, whom he described as being 'by far the best preacher among the Protestant divines', and appointed the bishop as his right-hand supporter at the coronation.[2]

Thomas Ken and four of his colleagues were later to be deprived of their sees for refusing to swear the oath of loyalty to William and Mary. But loyalty was already much on the minds of all six bishops as, having travelled the short distance upriver, they were shown into the royal presence and humbly presented their petition. James read it and immediately paled with rage (a reaction that was becoming all too familiar). 'This is a great surprise to me; here are strange words. I did not expect this from you! This is a standard of rebellion!' he exclaimed angrily. The bishops' protestations of fundamental loyalty were brushed aside and they were peremptorily dismissed with the king's words ringing in their ears:

> Is this what I have deserved, who have supported the Church of England and will support it? I will remember you that have signed this paper! ... I <u>will</u> be obeyed in publishing my Declaration ... God hath given me this dispensing power, and I will maintain it![3]

That same night – which must have been rather sleepless for those caught up in the drama – James' fury increased still further when he learned that the contents of the petition had already been leaked and were being openly hawked through the streets, taverns and coffee houses of London.

On 8 June all seven bishops including this time the archbishop were rounded up and again escorted to Whitehall, where they found themselves paraded like naughty schoolboys before a meeting of the Privy Council chaired by James. Still smarting from what he perceived to be their rebellious behaviour, the king ordered the bishops to explain themselves. They politely refused. Archbishop Sancroft made a dignified protest: 'Sir, we appear before you this day by virtue of your summons as criminals; the first time that ever I stood as a criminal before any man, and I am sorry that it happens to be before my sovereign lord.'[4] They were then told that they would be sent for trial at the court of King's Bench, charged with seditious libel. Lord Chancellor Jeffreys tried to get them to put up bail on their own recognizances, but again they refused, pleading their status as peers of the realm. There was nothing for it but to send them to gaol, and so they were once more loaded into boats and transported to the Tower, amidst scenes of popular support that boded ill for James.

At the Tower they were given all the comforts that their circumstances allowed, and received a constant stream of eminent visitors. These included John Evelyn, who had already noted their progress to the

Tower, 'infinite crowds of people on their knees, begging their blessing and praying for them as they passed out of the barge'. Bail was eventually arranged for all the accused on 15 June, no fewer than twenty-three noblemen standing surety.[5]

Fortunately the bishops had not long to wait. Their trial took place in Westminster Hall on 29 June and lasted all day. Argument between prosecution and defence surged mainly around questions of the legality or otherwise of the royal dispensing powers, and of the bishops' right to petition their king. (One of the witnesses was Samuel Pepys, who had been present at the Council meeting on 8 June; he successfully managed to stonewall the few questions put to him.)[6] The partisan attitude of the onlookers in the court (which at that time occupied a corner of the huge Hall) and the surging crowds outside did not make the work of the prosecution any easier. Government supporters present in court were subjected to jeers and insults, Lord Sunderland himself not only being threatened but soundly kicked up the backside as he passed through the throng in the Hall.[7] At the end of the day the four judges, who included Lord Chief Justice Robert Wright, gave individual summings-up (two for, two against), and the jury then retired. They did not reappear until about ten o'clock the following morning, when a verdict of not guilty was returned, 'at which there were several great shouts in court, and throughout the Hall'.[8] It was typical of James' sometimes vindictive nature that the two judges who spoke out against the Crown were speedily dismissed.

Once the verdict was known, thousands of people rejoiced in the streets and churches throughout the land, soldiers cheered, bells pealed, bonfires roared and a commemorative medal was struck. In contrast, an ominous hush pervaded the galleries and state rooms of Whitehall as the king and his ministers digested these latest developments. James now at last recognised that in prosecuting the bishops he had made a serious mistake. Having relied quite heavily on the established Church to support his moves towards toleration (always a doubtful prospect at the best of times), he had alienated the Church still further by pursuing his vendetta against the bishops as far as a court case which, humiliatingly, he had then lost. Moreover, to his chagrin, not only Anglicans but Dissenters, Non-conformists and even Scottish Presbyterians voiced their support for the bishops, who were seen to be champions of the general Protestant cause.[9] It was from this point onwards that James' authority may be said to have begun its final decline.

It is said that even the king's closest advisors, including Sunderland, Jeffreys and the Jesuit Father Petre, had entertained serious doubts on the wisdom of taking on the Anglican Church as personified by the bishops.[10] The opposing view taken by apologists for James is that he was persuaded by Jeffreys to do so.[11] However, there were other powerful figures at hand whose opposition to James and his policies was now translated from theoretical discussion into positive action. By coincidence, on the very same day as the seven bishops' acquittal another group of seven, this time composed of prominent but disaffected personalities, wrote to William of Orange in the name of the people, inviting him to mount an invasion of England and sort out the situation.

This group comprised the earls of Devonshire, Danby – not long released from the Tower – and Shrewsbury; Lord Lumley; the disgraced Bishop of London Henry Compton; and the unnobled but influential Admiral William Russell and Henry Sidney (later Earl of Romney). It had no mandate as such to approach William, but was sufficiently representative both of public opinion and of political unity to be taken seriously. Furthermore, although the letter had only seven signatures, it is certain that many more individuals in and around Government and court circles knew of it and endorsed it. The signatories (who became known as 'the Immortal Seven') assured William that once he had landed he could expect all the support he needed from 'the nobility and gentry', who between them would soon be able to raise an army in support of his invasion force. The people, they reported, 'are so generally dissatisfied with the present conduct of the Government in relation to their religion, liberties and properties … that your Highness may be assured there are nineteen parts of twenty of the people throughout the kingdom who are desirous of a change'.[12]

What is also certain is that the letter came as no great surprise to William. According to Burnet, as far back as April he had told Admiral Russell that if he were to be specifically invited into England by 'some men of the best interest, and the most valued in the nation ... he believed he could be ready by the end of September to come over'. His earlier apparent support for Monmouth, and his subsequent lukewarm support for James, coupled with his outright refusal to approve any moves towards repealing the Test Act, ought to have alerted the king to possible danger ahead. However, James blithely ignored the signals and continued to believe that his son-in-law, though unlovable, was basically 'sound' if perhaps a bit boring. Meanwhile William had quietly strengthened his contacts with dissidents in London and had built up a core of support formed by anti-Catholics and the politically disgruntled. In the end it was one event above all others that finally tipped the balance and propelled him into making active preparations to mount an invasion of England. After bearing a sad succession of children, all of whom died in infancy or soon after, James' wife had finally presented her incredulous though grateful husband with a healthy son and heir.

James Francis Edward, who would one day be known as 'the Old Pretender', was born on 10 June, just as the seven bishops were getting used to their new surroundings in the Tower. (One of his godfathers was also his Father in God, Pope Innocent XI – who, however, died the following year.) The Prince's birth, it may be assumed, helped to take his father's mind off the trial and its ramifications. Moreover, despite his various set-backs, James had never wavered in his belief that Divine Providence was ultimately on his side, and the birth of his son only confirmed him in this belief. But on the other hand it also helped to concentrate William's mind wonderfully. He was certainly heartened by the news that the royal birth had been received with muted interest if not indifference, despite James' efforts to whip up public enthusiasm. A few bonfires were lit, a few loyal addresses presented, perhaps a few hundred glasses and tankards raised, otherwise – nothing. The bishops had grabbed all the popular headlines.

Far more serious for James, and conversely encouraging for William, was a persistent rumour that the 'birth' had been a put-up job, that the child was an imposter, and that it had been smuggled into the queen's bed in a warming-pan. Certainly a warming-pan had been used, as was testified some months later by Margaret Dawson, one of the queen's women of the bedchamber, who stated 'that she saw fire carried into the Queen's room in a warming-pan to warm the bed, after which the Queen went into her bed, and that [she] stirred not from the Queen until her Majesty was delivered of a son'.[13] Gossip about the alleged shady dealings surrounding the birth grew ever stronger, prompting Mary, Princess of Orange, to write to her sister Princess Anne on 21 July, asking for a full report on the affair. She had already received a letter from Anne (18 June), in which the princess, referring to her stepmother, grudgingly granted that 'it is possible it may be her child,' but followed this up with the forthright assertion, 'where one believes it, a thousand do not. For my part … I shall ever be of the number of unbelievers.' It was obviously with some glee that she wrote again three weeks later (9 July) with the news that 'The Prince of Wales has been ill these three or four days … I believe it will not be long before he is an angel in heaven.'[14] (In fact James Edward outlived Anne by fifty-two years.)

Mary's claim to the throne was now seriously threatened by the unwelcome arrival of her new half-brother. She will certainly not have echoed the sentiments conveyed in James' note to her husband announcing the happy event: 'The Queen was, God be thanked, safely delivered of a son on Sunday morning, a little after ten.'[15] It was therefore in the joint interests of herself and her husband to foster the warming-pan *canard* and to join the ranks of those who denied the fledgling Prince any shred of legitimacy.

Having thus shown his hand, William began to make positive preparations for an invasion although, as we have seen, he had already begun to contemplate the possibilities as early as the spring. It must be recognised that his concerns were not prompted solely by domestic politics in England, but also by his fear that, unless the situation was stabilised, there could be serious international repercussions. Almost certainly there would be further opportunities for mischief-making by Louis XIV, whose spectre as always loomed large over Europe, and who was now trying to dominate some of the many small German states. If James prevailed he might enter into Catholic collusion with Louis and side with him in another attack on the Netherlands. If on the other hand there was to be another civil war in England, the ensuing chaos would ensure that William could not expect help from that quarter in the event of a French threat or even assault; worse, such a situation could also actively encourage Louis in his aggressive intent.[16]

William calculated that, were he to carry out his invasion, Louis would be too engrossed in his current German adventure to help James. Nevertheless William took care to secure his home borders by making protective arrangements with the various neighbouring German states, in particular Brandenburg, where the Elector Frederick (later King of Prussia) was also William's heir. In addition Frederick promised to provide several thousand extra troops for the invasion, as did other German rulers.[17] An interesting series of notes in William's own hand, preserved amongst the State Papers, shows that he also hoped to get financial support from these states: *Obtain money from Saxony, Brandenburg, Cell[e], Hanover, Wolfenbuttel, Wirtemberg, Hesse-Cassel.*[18]

At home William had also to gain the approval of the States-General before embarking on the invasion. The rich burghers of the Dutch cities such as Haarlem, Delft and above all Amsterdam were not greatly interested in England's religious or political problems. What really did interest them was trade, which because of the ongoing Dutch-French feuding was in decline. The prospect of James continuing to rule in England was alarming, for the Netherlands literally could not afford to allow Louis XIV the luxury of another pro-Catholic ally who might gang up with him against them and ruin their trade prospects completely. When the facts were put before the members of the States-General they eventually overcame their initial reluctance to get involved with the invasion and on the very eve of William's departure, and despite warnings from Louis not to interfere, voted to support it (28 October OS).[19]

The weeks were passing and winter was approaching. For William, time was clearly of the essence, but for James it was a vital commodity which he did not have. However, despite all the warnings which he was now beginning to receive, he still could not bring himself to believe that William would actually invade. On the contrary, he reasoned that troop movements in the Netherlands were all to do with the unstable situation in Europe, where Louis had now declared war on the Hapsburg Emperor Leopold I and had entered Germany across the Rhine on 27 September (NS). So for a short time James continued with his scheme to hold an election for a Parliament packed with his supporters and primed to repeal the Test Act. But it was not to be; reports from his agents in the Netherlands finally convinced him that the situation really was becoming dangerous, and so all preparations for the election were swiftly abandoned.

Unfounded rumours were already beginning to spread. On 18 September John Evelyn went from his Greenwich home up to London, 'where I found the Court in the utmost consternation upon report of the Pr of Oranges landing, which put Whitehall into so panic a feare, that I could hardly believe it possible to find such a change'. There had as yet been no such landing, but the possibility was now openly acknowledged, and James belatedly began to assemble his own forces.

During the two summers in which it had been encamped on Hounslow Heath, the army had got used to its surroundings and daily routine, so much so that, despite improvements in drill and training, its effectiveness in the face of the sudden new challenge was somewhat in doubt. In other words, it had, some thought, gone soft. Its loyalties were also giving cause for alarm; for example, sections of it had shown unwelcome enthusiasm for the seven bishops and their recent acquittal. It was not large enough to meet the demands of the moment, and reinforcements were urgently needed. Accordingly recruitment (some voluntary, some not) was stepped up, and extra troops were summoned from both Ireland and Scotland. Horses were also commandeered. The exact numbers of troops vary from one account to another, but the Irish contingent seems to have totalled about 3,000 men and the Scottish, about 1,000 more.

Social problems were posed by the Irish, who as a Catholic military presence were regarded inevitably with suspicion by the populace in general. (It was specifically ordered that 'the troops which are to come for England [from Ireland] bring no wives or other women with them'.)[20] The final tally of James' army was probably somewhere between 35,000 and 40,000. The militia was not a factor; owing to James' aversion to it and to the disturbed state of local government prior to the expected election, it had been allowed to fall into a state of almost total unreadiness, and was not expected to contribute to the emergency in any significant way.

As the troops assembled over the days and weeks, James was also active on the home front. A royal proclamation issued on 28 September stated that the vicious criticisms of the king for his alleged attacks on religion and personal liberty were merely a cloak for the intended invasion, and all citizens were ordered to arm themselves in readiness for the approaching conflict. On the same date a representative selection of six bishops, including four of those recently on trial (but not Archbishop Sancroft), was summoned to meet the king at Whitehall, where he announced his intention of letting bygones be bygones, although apparently without going into too much detail. Two days later he had a private interview with the archbishop, and on 3 October he again received the archbishop, who was now accompanied by eight colleagues, namely, the bishops of London (Henry Compton's re-instatement having been agreed by James), Winchester, Ely, Chichester, Bath and Wells, Peterborough, Bristol and St Asaph. William Sancroft first addressed the king in measured tones of rebuke:

> May it please your sacred Majesty: When I had lately the honour to wait upon you, you were pleased briefly to acquaint me with what had passed two days before between your Majesty and these my reverend bretheren; by which ... I perceived that in truth there passed nothing, but in very general terms, and expressions of your Majesty's gracious and favourable inclinations towards the Church of England, and of our reciprocal duty and loyalty to your Majesty; both of which were sufficiently understood and declared before.

He then set out in some detail, under ten separate heads, the various reforms which the bishops wished to see carried out. These included:

> That your Majesty will be graciously pleased to annul your Commission for Ecclesiastical Affairs [Head 2] ... That you will ... restore the President and Fellows of St. Mary Magdalene College in Oxford [Head 3] ... That your Majesty will ... desist from the exercise of such a dispensing power

as hath of late been used; and to permit that point to be freely and calmly debated, argued, and finally settled in Parliament [Head 4] ... Above all, that your Majesty will ... permit your bishops to offer you such motives and arguments as (we trust) may by God's grace ... persuade your Majesty to return to the communion of the Church of England [Head 10].

The bishops also asked the king to call *a free and regular Parliament* as soon as possible – but the time for this had already passed.

James' reaction was uncharacteristically subdued. As one commentator put it, 'The proposals would at another time have raised the king's indignation, but the necessity of his affairs obliged him now to thank their lordships, and to promise that he would comply with them.' The promise was doubtless made through gritted teeth and with a forced smile. However, over the next fortnight he went some way towards meeting the bishops' requests. In a series of announcements the hated Commission was dissolved (5 October), the affairs of Magdalen College were ordered to be settled 'regularly and statutably' (10 October), and most of the various corporation charters, which had been meddled with in the attempt to elect a packed Parliament, were to be restored (as requested by the bishops in Head 8 of their list). For good measure James also decreed the removal from their posts of 'all mayors, sheriffs, recorders, town-clerks, aldermen, common-councilmen &c which had been put in by the late king or by his present majesty, ever since the year 1679', although it is difficult to judge to what extent this sweeping instruction was actually carried out.[21]

Another casualty was Lord Sunderland, who on 27 October was suddenly deprived of his posts of Lord President of the Council and Secretary of State. The reasons for his dismissal were not fully understood at the time, and remain something of a mystery, but it seems that the king – still smarting from the outcome of the bishops' trial – had finally lost faith in the earl's judgement and political acumen. Quite simply, 'My Lord Sunderland was not the man he took him for, nor any longer to be trusted.' Nevertheless James himself announced that Sunderland's loyalty was not in doubt nor was he suspected of treasonable correspondence, but he shed no further light on the affair.[22]

In fact James' belated attempts to re-ingratiate himself with the Church of England were too little and had come far too late. On 16 October Archbishop Sancroft received a further summons to Whitehall where, after some general discussion, 'at last the King came to … his chief intention in sending for the Archbishop [which was] to tell him that he had received certain intelligence, that the Prince of Orange was coming to invade England, and to make a conquest of it'.[23] James could already have seen a copy of an official document published in The Hague on 30 September (10 October NS) and entitled *The Declaration of His Highness William Henry, by the grace of God Prince of Orange &c, of the Reasons inducing him to Appear in Arms in the Kingdom of England.*[24] The 'Reasons' were all the usual points of conflict – the powers of suspending and dispensing, the advancement of Catholics, the Magdalen College affair, the interference with civic charters, the attempts to rig elections, etc. etc. Nevertheless William was careful not to point the finger of accusation directly at James, but instead to lay the blame at the door of a bunch of unnamed scheming ministers. He did, however, entirely reject the legitimacy of James' new heir. An *Additional Declaration* was appended on 24 October (NS).

Of all the myriad problems besetting the king at this crucial time, the question of the legitimacy was one of those which he found the most troubling. Aware of the persistent rumours and also of the powerful effect of William's propaganda, James determined on a grand gesture which – he hoped – would settle the matter once and for all. On 22 October he convened at Whitehall an 'Extraordinary Council', which was indeed extraordinary for its size and composition. Almost one hundred people were summoned; they included the Queen Dowager, Prince George of Denmark (husband of Princess Anne, who was conveniently absent due to one of her many unsuccessful pregnancies), forty-two noblemen, six bishops, some twenty judges and other lawyers including Roger North in his capacity as the queen's Attorney-General, and the Lord Mayor and aldermen of the City.[25] Once all were assembled in the Council Chamber, the king made his purpose clear:

My Lords: I have called you together upon a very extraordinary occasion; but extraordinary diseases must have extraordinary remedies. The malicious

endeavours of my enemies have so poisoned the minds of some of my subjects, that … I have reason to believe that very many do not think this son,
with which God has blessed me, to be mine, but a supposed child. But I
may say, that … scarce any prince was ever born, where there were so many
persons present. I have taken this time to have the matter heard and exam-
ined here, expecting that the Prince of Orange, with the first easterly wind,
will invade this kingdom.

After James had spoken, a procession of forty witnesses, ranging from Lord
Chancellor Jeffreys to the queen's laundress Elizabeth Pearse, deposed that
they had either been in the bedroom, some also having assisted in the
birth, or had been waiting outside and had been called in immediately
after the birth had taken place. When all had said their piece the king
wound up the proceedings: 'And now, my Lords, although I did not question but that every person here present was satisfied before in this matter,
yet by what you have heard, you will be better able to satisfy others.'[26]

Despite this comment, some doubters did undoubtedly attend the meeting, but it is impossible to say how many were convinced by the evidence
put before them. The king's position was further undermined by William's
well-oiled propaganda machine which had now arranged for thousands of
copies of the *Declaration* to be distributed in England. On 2 November
some of the bishops received yet another summons to Whitehall, where
James informed them that one of William's agents had been caught in the
act of distributing copies, and that he himself 'had received five or six copies
from several persons, to whom they had been sent in penny post letters,
which he had thrown into the fire'. At this meeting and several subsequent
ones, James tried hard to get the bishops' agreement that they would pub-
lish a denunciation of the *Declaration*, especially William's claim that he had
been invited to invade 'by a great many of the lords both temporal and
spiritual'. No doubt with an eye to the possible future, as well as recognition
of the folly of getting mixed up in politics again (a point which Archbishop
Sancroft boldly made to the king), the bishops always managed to side-step
the issue. Eventually James gave up on this particular point, crossly declaring
that, 'I will urge you no further. If you will not assist me as I desire, I must
stand upon my own legs, and trust to myself, and my own arms.'[27]

In general the sorely tried bishops tried to remain impartial. Nevertheless there were many laymen who looked forward to the invasion with positive enthusiasm, including a sizeable body of exiled Whig and other noblemen and gentlemen who had been lurking in the Netherlands for some months, waiting for just this opportunity.[28] Meanwhile in England itself a group of powerful but devious noblemen had kept up a clandestine correspondence with William at least since May, assuring him of their loyalty if and when he should land. They included the Immortal Seven, plus the Marquis of Halifax, the Earl of Nottingham and Lord Bath.[29]

Anti-Catholic riots in various cities including London grew progressively more violent as the crisis deepened, the prime targets in most centres being Catholic chapels, their personnel and their contents. What happened in Norwich on 14 October was fairly typical. Writing to Lord Sunderland, the Duke of Norfolk reported that on visiting the city he had 'learned of a great disorder that happened yesterday (Sunday) at the Catholic chapel. The rabble were very insolent there in the morning, and they [the congregation] desired the Mayor to send some guard to protect them in the afternoon ... He and the Sheriffs went and dispersed the rabble, who were judged to be 1,000, though most [were] boys.'[30]

SPREADING THE NEWS

In these days of multi-media twenty-four-hour coverage of world events, news is almost instantaneous. Clearly it was not so in the seventeenth century. So how on earth, as the events of the Glorious Revolution gradually unfolded, did anyone find out what was really going on?

For those who lived in remote parts of the country it was often many weeks before the facts became known, and when they did they were often wildly inaccurate and misleading. The first hint of anything happening might be brought as hearsay by pedlars or other itinerants. In market towns the crier – with the aid of his bell and the stentorian voice which had won him his job – would make official announcements on the orders of his employers, the town council. Companies of strolling players, performing in barns or inn courtyards, might bring snippets of news which they had picked up en route. Ballad singers intoned musical reports of events, and supplemented their efforts with crudely printed woodcuts which illustrated the songs. Even the vicar, often better informed and certainly more literate than many of his parishioners, might refer in his sermons to far-distant developments which could affect them all. Sometimes, indeed, he himself became the mouthpiece of authority, as when incumbents were ordered by King James to read the 1688 Declaration of Indulgence from their pulpits.

But perhaps most importantly, there were also letters. The Penny Post is often thought of as a nineteenth-century development – not so. In fact a countrywide postal service had existed since 1635, when on the orders of Charles I the official General Post Office was established by Thomas Witherings, a merchant and entrepreneur. Witherings' instructions were to set up a regular postal service between London and Edinburgh, guaranteed to complete the return journey in six days. To speed things up, new roads were built, including the Great West and Great North roads, and post offices were opened at regular intervals along the routes; here horses and men were kept in readiness for each change-over, supervised by the postmaster. A network of minor roads branching out from the main routes ensured that mail could also reach outlying towns and villages, and postage was paid by the recipient.

The charge was 2d per sheet for the first 80 miles, double for two sheets. This was expensive, and so most addressees did not welcome over-long letters. Moreover, while the system worked well for the country in general, it had a major flaw in that it concentrated on sending letters out of London and did nothing to help circulate them within the capital and its suburbs. In 1680 another businessman, William Dockwra, solved the problem by floating the first Penny Post for London, concentrated within a 10-mile radius of the capital. This scheme – which retained the feature of payment on receipt – soon made such a favourable impact that Dockwra sought and obtained a patent for it. But he had reckoned without James, Duke of York. The duke had obtained a monopoly on the profits from the General Post Office, and fully intended that he should also benefit from the Penny Post. Dockwra was not only relieved of his patent but also heavily fined for having had the impudence to apply for it in the first place.

London did not have post offices. Instead it had coffee houses, which performed the same function. It was here that letters were collected and sorted, here that messengers (postmen) reported on an hourly basis, and from here that they set off on their rounds. Coffee houses first appeared in London in the early 1650s, and by 1663 they numbered about eighty. They at once became popular as places where gentlemen (never ladies) could meet to discuss politics, business, news from abroad and lots of gossip over the coffee cups. The events of 1688–89 would have provided exactly the kind of information, garbled or otherwise, on which the coffee houses flourished, although most patrons were under no illusions as to the accuracy of the various reports going the rounds. 'Though there never was more occasion of inquiry for busy impertinent people that gad about all day long for coffee and news, yet never was less certainty of what passes in the world.' So wrote Samuel de Paz, Lord Dartmouth's Spanish secretary, to a friend in Ireland in November 1688.[31]

Sometimes the authorities became alarmed that some coffee houses had become hotbeds of rebellion and places where anti-Government plots were laid, and there was talk of closing them down. However, these threats never came to anything and the coffee houses continued to flour-ish. Samuel Pepys had hardly begun his famous *Diary* on 1 January 1660 before, on 9 January, he was reporting a visit to a coffee house where he paid 18d to become a member of a political club which regularly met there. Coffee houses had distinctive names such as the Turk's Head, Lloyd's, and Garraway's. (In time Lloyd's evolved into the famous shipping underwriters; Garraway's is mentioned in *The Pickwick Papers* and finally closed in 1866.)

Two other sources of news deserve mention here, and both were regularly circulated at the coffee houses. First, the pamphlet. Throughout the seventeenth century, pamphlets were a highly influential political weapon and played a considerable part in shaping public opinion, just as television, newspapers and other media outlets do today. They were often anonymous, and most were produced in London by licensed printers, who operated mainly from the capital and whose numbers were severely restricted by law. It is said that when William of Orange arrived in Exeter and wanted copies of his *Declaration* run off, not a single printer could be found in the city to do the job. Pamphlets were sold cheaply by street vendors or could be bought in print shops, and they also found their way by various means throughout the rest of the country. Single copies could be posted up in town and village centres for those who could read, and they would then pass on the information to those who could not.

Second, newspapers. In 1695 the suspension of the Licensing Act, which until then had greatly restricted the activities of printers, led to the expansion of newspapers which so far had not been much different from pamphlets. This expansion came too late to cover the events of 1688–89, but newspapers such as the *London Gazette* or the *Flying Post* made up for it in their vigorous examination of the policies and events that marked the later years of King William's reign.

Meanwhile in the Netherlands William had been gradually assembling his troops and transports ready for the invasion. Estimates of the number of soldiers involved have varied widely over the years, but latest research suggests a figure somewhere between 12,000 and 15,000. William himself had assumed a total of 20,000, in a handwritten note whose date of July 1688 shows that his plans were already well advanced.[32] Only a relatively small proportion of the men were Dutch; the rest were mercenaries from a wide variety of countries including England itself, Scotland, Ireland, Germany, Switzerland and Sweden. There were also (oddly) some Laplanders, and 200 colourfully-dressed warriors from the colony of Dutch Guiana (Surinam).[33] Whatever the correct total, it is certain that James' army was considerably larger, perhaps 40,000 men, of which the main body of some 30,000 was now brought together and concentrated on Salisbury Plain, the remainder being distributed between various key garrison points throughout the country.[34]

On paper an army of this size should have been more than capable of dealing with the invasion. Moreover the approach of winter was already being signalled by bad weather, which was usually enough to make most military commanders of the day think twice before venturing out on campaign. Despite all the evidence to the contrary James, whilst continuing to prepare for conflict, still wanted to believe that William was too astute a tactician and too seasoned a general to launch the invasion in such conditions. Neither could he conceive that at such a notoriously bad time of year William would leave his own country exposed so seriously to possible French attack, regardless of the promises of help offered by the various German states. But for his part William, whilst fully recognising the risks involved, also knew that they could work to his advantage, in that the invasion would be that much more unexpected. There was to be no further delay. On Friday 29 October (NS), aboard his ship the frigate *Den Briel* and with his standard bravely fluttering at the stern, William led his armada out from the assembly port of Hellevoetsluis onto the heaving seas, in the direction of England.

The general direction, that is, for the Dutch fleet was to a large extent at the mercy of the winds. This soon became all too clear when the easterly wind which had been blowing suddenly changed to a westerly gale so severe that the ships had to return to port for shelter. The main casualties of this buffeting were many unfortunate horses, perhaps about 1,000. It is said that the majority of these deaths resulted from suffocation below decks; however, it is also probable that some suffered injuries on the pitching transports, and that others were swept from the decks to a watery death in the boiling seas. Weather conditions then changed, so that late in the day on 11 November the fleet was able to set off again, this time carried forward on a strong easterly breeze which was later to be known as 'the Protestant wind', and was taken by the pious as a sign of Divine approval. On 13 November the Dutch ships passed through the Straits of Dover and into the English Channel in a massed formation clearly visible from the chalky clifftops, with the same kind of brazen assurance that they had displayed when sailing up the Medway in 1667.

They certainly made a brave show. About fifty warships shepherded a motley collection of troop transports, supply ships and landing craft, made up from typical Dutch sailing vessels with musical-sounding names such as the fluyt and galiot. In civilian use the fluyt was a three-masted, square-rigged merchant ship of up to 300 tonnes which could carry a large cargo but needed only a small crew, while the galiot (galliot, galioot, galyoot, galjoot) could have from one to three masts and was also of 300 tonnes. Both were rather squat in appearance and were rounded at bow and stern. Other ship-types which may have been used were the two-masted dogger (a fishing boat) and the tjalk, also two-masted but with a flat bottom – and therefore very suitable as a landing craft. Apart from the tjalk all these ships had shallow draughts. The total number of ships involved was probably slightly over 450, although some estimates are higher.

As the fleet, laden with tired and seasick soldiers, stoical sailors and restive horses, sailed purposefully along the English coastline, on land there was enormous confusion about William's intentions and especially where he might be intending to come ashore. Yorkshire (perhaps Hull?), Essex, the east coast, the West Country – all, it was thought, could be possible, especially as the weather had successfully tied down the navy, under its aptly named commander Admiral Lord Dartmouth, in the offshore anchorage known as the Gunfleet, near the Essex coast and today's seaside resorts of Clacton and Frinton. (Dartmouth, a Catholic, had replaced Admiral Herbert, who had earlier defected to William and was now leading the Dutch fleet.) Originally William himself was in some doubt as to where he should aim: 'Whether to disembark in several places or one? If it is necessary to make a simultaneous descent on Scotland? Act according to events,' he had written in his notes back in July.[35] In the end his chosen anchorage – partly dictated by the winds and tides – was Torbay, and he first set foot on land at Brixham, a previously unnoticed Devon fishing village. (In 1989, in an imaginative gesture towards its historical importance, Torbay was twinned with Hellevoetsluis.) But if the place of William's arrival was obscure, the date was much less so – 5 November, a day whose potentially disastrous significance was still strongly felt eighty-three years after the uncovering of the Gunpowder Plot.

Amongst the entourage setting foot on the wet and slippery stones of Brixham harbour were two of William's closest advisors. First was Hans Willem (William) van Bentinck, a close friend of William since boyhood and privy to all his secrets, so much so that in time English politicians and courtiers came to resent his influence. They also envied the favours shown to him and the wealth showered upon him by a grateful William. He was sent on various diplomatic and military missions and was created Earl of Portland.

Second was Gilbert Burnet, a learned but affable Scots theologian who, whilst travelling in Europe, had (in the eyes of King James) become suspiciously friendly with William and Mary, and was consequently not welcome at home. Not surprisingly he then switched his allegiance and was eventually appointed William's chaplain for the expedition to England. But there is evidence to show that before then he had already become politically influential at The Hague. He had forged links on behalf of William with the disaffected Whig plotters in London, and had helped William and Mary to formulate their policies, e.g. by advising them to oppose the repeal of the Test Act. He had also developed a highly efficient propaganda machine which, by means of pamphlets, official declarations and even pro-Williamite sermons, vigorously punched home the message that William's crusade enjoyed Divine support and approval.[36]

However, it is Burnet's literary work that has endured, especially his *History of My Own Time* (begun 1683). This is a valuable if sometimes biased record of events covering the period from 1603 to 1715, written in a chatty and attractive style that is still very readable today.[37] Burnet delivered the sermon at the coronation on 11 April 1689 as Bishop of Salisbury, to which office he had just been appointed.

James probably first got confirmation of William's unchallenged arrival on the day following the landing. It is said that he actually received the news in the studio of the court painter Godfrey Kneller whilst sitting for a portrait which had been commissioned by the faithful Samuel Pepys, and which Pepys later hung in his own library.[38] At first uncertain how to react, James eventually concluded that the best strategy in the circumstances would be to concentrate his forces on and around Salisbury Plain, where much of the army was already encamped, and to make a stand against William, cutting off any further advances, whether west or north or towards London itself. Once again the tried and tested military duo of Lord Feversham and Lieutenant-General John Churchill were respectively appointed Commander-in-Chief and second-in-command – though Churchill's appointment was a last-minute move, ratified only on 7 November – and were despatched to Salisbury.[39] (At the same time the politically devious Churchill was the most noteworthy of a group of disaffected officers who for several months had been secretly plotting to go over to William's side should he seem to be prevailing.)[40] Both were issued from supplies with ceremonial suits of armour; Feversham's had been originally made for Charles II, Churchill's for James himself.[41]

James himself followed his generals on 17 [19?] November via Windsor and Basingstoke, arriving at Salisbury two days later.[42] Given the already appalling rutted and muddy state of the roads and the damp, biting chill of an early winter (it was actually blowing a blizzard as he reached Salisbury), he had made good speed. But it was already too late to stop the rot. By now William was encamped in Exeter, which he entered on a white horse at the head of an impressive cavalcade. Here his tired troops were welcomed with enthusiasm and were able to find rest and refreshment, although the mayor was lukewarm and the cathedral dignitaries were conspicuous by their absence. By now also a steady trickle of desertions from James' army had begun. For William there had been a disappointing reluctance by the local Devonshire gentry to declare their support for him, and recruitment in general had been slow – but these attitudes were perhaps linked to painful memories of the Monmouth rebellion and its aftermath.[43] More typical was a kind of passive 'wait and see' attitude while the population looked on and judged what the outcome might be, unwilling to commit itself at this stage to either side.

Thus suddenly faced with impending disaster and the need for swift, decisive action, James reacted strongly. He suffered a tremendous nosebleed and retired to bed in his well-appointed tent. There can be little doubt that this attack – which was followed intermittently by others – was psychosomatic (even some of his own doctors thought so), but it was no less severe for that, and it was three days – time that could be ill afforded – before James was fit enough to face up fully to the demands of the deteriorating situation. (However, on the plus side there were rumours that a plot to kidnap him had been forestalled by his indisposition.)[44] Things were certainly not looking good. Desertions continued, though still at a low level, but the most serious news to date was that William had finally left Exeter and had advanced into the countryside as far as Sherborne, almost 40 miles further on.[45] At a council of war James listened gloomily to conflicting advice from his commanders. Churchill urged the need to stand firm and give battle, but the more cautious Feversham advised the king to fall back towards London, and it was his advice that James finally followed, ordering a retreat to the Thames-side town of Marlow.[46] For John Churchill this was the final straw. On the night of 23/24 November he left his encampment together with James' nephew the Duke of Grafton and a troop of several hundred cavalry, and rode to join William at Axminster.[47] Next day James received news that his son-in-law Prince George of Denmark, the Duke of Ormonde, the Duke of Northumberland and others had also defected. In an ironic reflection of James' own state of health, the seepage of desertions had become a serious haemorrhage.

6

OUT WITH THE OLD,
IN WITH THE NEW

The news of Churchill's defection cast a long shadow over James' preparations for an orderly retreat back to London. His gloomy, mud-spattered cavalcade stopped off at Andover, from where he sent word to Lord Dartmouth to prepare for the arrival of the infant Prince of Wales who, in the event of a final catastrophe, should then be taken across to France.[1] The Prince, cocooned in his cot and sublimely unaware of the drama swirling around him, was already at the heavily fortified base of Portsmouth under the temporary guardianship of trusted Catholic supporters, Lord and Lady Powis.

After Andover James then trundled on towards London, arriving back at Whitehall on 26 November. More bad news awaited him. His daughter Anne, her friend Lady Sarah Churchill and the Bishop of London had all hurriedly left town together in the early hours of the morning heading north to Nottingham, where there was a strong body of opposition headed by the Earl of Devonshire. Booted, spurred and well-armed, Bishop Compton relished the chance to re-live his earlier days (he had once been a dragoon).[2] The two women had escaped arrest – ordered by James – by the narrowest of margins. A fortnight later, on the instructions of William, Anne joined her husband Prince George in Oxford, and on 19 December they arrived back in Whitehall.[3] Her defence throughout was her unswerving loyalty to the Church of

England and her detestation of popery in any shape or form, an attitude deeply instilled into her by Compton, who had long been her spiritual mentor. (Back in 1676 it had been he, as the spiritual guardian of Anne and her elder sister Mary, who had decided that they were ready for confirmation; their father had forbidden it but had been overruled by his brother the king.) But the base ingratitude and disloyalty of it all affected James deeply. 'God help me! Even my children have forsaken me,' was his reported, anguished reaction. His sense of betrayal would have been even more acute had he known that as early as 18 November Anne had sent a message to William informing him that her husband (and, by implication, herself) intended to join the opposition.[4]

In London and other cities anti-Catholic disturbances continued to grow in frequency and intensity. Once again mobs roamed the streets looting, pillaging and burning Catholic properties and possessions, and often could be controlled only by the wholesale use of militia and regular troops. More orderly and generally bloodless changes had already taken place in large areas of the Midland and northern counties, organised by an alliance of dissident noblemen who had long been opposed to James and his policies and were backed by their own military forces. On 22 November, after weeks of planning, the resurgent Earl of Danby had taken over the symbolically important city of York, in the name of 'a free Parliament and the Protestant religion, and no popery!'[5] The equally important city and port of Hull, always a strategic prize, fell to him soon afterwards. Danby in fact 'had given the greatest shock to the King's authority in the North of any that appear'd against it'.[6] The East Anglian centres of Norwich and King's Lynn were occupied by the Duke of Norfolk. Nottingham was under the control of Lord Devonshire, as has been shown, and in both Lancashire and Cheshire Lord Delamere had secured widespread support.

In all these places measures were taken to disarm, sometimes to arrest, and generally to neutralise Catholics. Before William's invasion, the existence of such substantial pockets of northern resistance had made it seem likely that the landing would actually be made somewhere in the North, so as to take advantage of the additional troops and facilities available there. However, events proved otherwise, perhaps partly because William preferred to do things his way without becoming embroiled in local politics or finding himself beholden to individual noblemen backed by private armies.

Meanwhile on 27 November, the day following his return to London, James held an emergency meeting of peers and advisors, to see whether anything could be salvaged from the wreckage of Government hopes and, more urgently, what steps if any could be taken to avert further catastrophe. The meeting was long, the discussions wide-ranging and sometimes heated. The plain-speaking Lord Clarendon (son of Charles II's disgraced Chancellor) summed up the situation with brutal clarity:

> Sir, it is a maxim in our law that the King can do no wrong, but his Ministers may, and be called to account for it too. Now in the present juncture of affairs, what would you have us do to appease the nation, since the people have been so provoked by the papists? ... When your Majesty was at Salisbury, you might have had some remedy, but the people do now say that the King is run away with his army; we are left defenceless and must therefore side with the prevailing party.[7]

Clarendon spoke from experience, aware that his own son had already joined William's ranks and that he himself was preparing to do the same.

In the end it was agreed that the best hope of progress, however unpromising, lay in summoning a new Parliament ('the only remedy in our present circumstances,' as Lord Rochester bleakly put it) to meet on 15 January, and that the necessary writs should be issued forthwith. It was also proposed that a Commission should be appointed to approach William and put out peace feelers. Their main message would be that, provided William would agree not to enter London, elections would indeed be held for a Parliament which should be in essence a talking-shop for the resolution of the current situation. On 29 November James appointed lords Halifax, Nottingham and Godolphin to this thank-less task, and on the same day the Earl of Feversham wrote to William informing him that the king 'intends to send Commissioners to treat with your Highness ... and that in order thereunto his Majesty desires you to send me passports in blank for his said Commissioners'.[8]

After several days' delay, caused partly by weather conditions which made travelling more than usually difficult, partly by military activity, the Commissioners finally reached William on 8 December at Hungerford near Newbury. Ahead of his camp the action swirled in and around Reading, where the main army's vanguard had met with fierce opposition from a body of Irish dragoons several hundred strong. There was considerable bloodshed and, although the Irish were inevitably routed, their resistance was a sharp reminder that, of all James' large army, throughout the campaign it had been the Irish troops who, with their fierce loyalty to the Catholic cause, had given James the most support and William the most trouble.[9]

By 10 December the Commissioners were back in town and soon reporting to James. Their message was that William basically approved the idea of elections, but had some conditions of his own. Amongst other things, he demanded a purge of papists and the right to join James on an equal footing in presiding over the sessions of the forthcoming Parliament. But by now all such matters were largely academic. For James knew that his queen had already fled to France with their son, and privately he was determined to follow her.

As November drew to a close James had decided that the time had come to instruct Lord Dartmouth to escort the Prince of Wales over to France. Unexpectedly the trusted Dartmouth refused, fearing an accusation of treason if he were to deliver the prince into the power of the French. However, aware of the dangerous situation, the Governor of Portsmouth, Lord Dover, and the baby prince's guardians had already taken matters into their own hands and had decided to return him to the care of his parents without further delay. Leaving Portsmouth on 8 December with their precious charge, Lord and Lady Powis reached London on the following day, despite facing many hazards en route.[10] The anxious parents received their infant child with joy, swiftly tempered by distress when it became clear that for safety's sake the queen would have to take him to France herself, without the support of her husband. No doubt tears were shed, but there was no help for it. Early on the morning of Monday 10 December, and with a handful of attendants, Mary crept out of Whitehall by a back door, carrying her child and disguised as a laundry-maid.

1 King James II, watercolour on vellum after Sir Godfrey Kneller, 1684/85. (National Portrait Gallery, London)

2 The Burning of HMS *Royal James* at the Battle of Solebay, 28 May 1672, by Willem van de Velde the Younger, late seventeenth century. (National Maritime Museum, Greenwich, London)

3 James, Duke of York and
Anne (Hyde), Duchess of
York, oil on canvas by Sir
Peter Lely, *c.* 1663. (National
Portrait Gallery, London)

4 Mary of Modena, oil on
canvas by Willem Wissing,
1685. (National Portrait
Gallery, London)

The INTHRONIZATION of Their MAJESTIES King IAMES the Second and Queen MARY.

5 The coronation of King James II and Queen Mary, engraving by W. Sherwin, 1685/87.
(The Trustees of the British Museum)

6 Titus Oates in the pillory outside Westminster Hall, oil on canvas by an unknown artist,
1687. (© Museum of London)

7 Henry Purcell, oil on canvas by or after John Closterman, 1695. (National Portrait Gallery, London)

8 James Scott, Duke of Monmouth and Buccleuch, oil on canvas after Willem Wissing, *c.* 1683. (National Portrait Gallery, London)

9 George Jeffreys, 1st Baron Jeffreys of Wem, mezzotint by Edward Cooper after Sir Godfrey Kneller, 1686. (National Portrait Gallery, London)

10 The Seven Bishops, oil on canvas by an unknown artist, c. 1688. (National Portrait Gallery, London)

11 King William III and Queen Mary, mezzotint by Wallerant Vaillant after an unknown artist, 1677. (National Portrait Gallery, London)

12 Interior of a London Coffee House, drawing by an unknown artist, *c.* 1690. (The Trustees of the British Museum)

13 William and Mary receiving the crown, engraving by James Parker after James Northcote, published 1790. (National Portrait Gallery, London)

14 A Frost Fair on the Thames at Temple Stairs, oil on canvas by Abraham Hondius, 1684. (© Museum of London)

15 William III at the Battle of the Boyne, oil on canvas by Jan Wyck, 1690. (© UK Government Art Collection)

16 The King's Grand Staircase (detail), Hampton Court, mural by Antonio Verrio, c. 1700. (© Historic Royal Palaces)

By evening the little party had reached Gravesend undetected and had boarded a small yacht, its use officially sanctioned by Samuel Pepys.[11] Setting sail immediately for France, they arrived safely at Calais on 11 December.

The king's own intention to leave England was not entirely personal, for it seems that he had already discussed the possibility with his advisors, as an alternative to a political or even a military solution. But James had little faith in a political resolution, based as it would be on the election of an unreliable Parliament, and even less on a military one, although even at this late hour his army could perhaps have regrouped, been reorganised and infused with fighting spirit by an inspired leader. James, however, was by now anything but inspired. Gone was the old decisiveness and careless bravery of the Duke of York, Lord High Admiral, to be replaced by a catastrophic loss of self-confidence and a defeatist attitude so out of character as to suggest some kind of mental breakdown.[12] In this situation it was hardly surprising that James chose to leave the country. Nevertheless it is important to recognise that apparently neither he nor his ministers looked on his withdrawal as a final abdication, more as an opportunity to take stock of events and start planning for a come-back which they hoped would be permanent.

On 11 December the Earl of Feversham wrote from his military headquarters at Uxbridge to Prince William, saying that he had received that morning a letter from the king 'with the unfortunate news of his resolution to go out of England and that he is actually gone'. Lord Feversham also reported that James had given orders expressly forbidding the army to put up any kind of resistance.[13] In fact the king left Whitehall very early on the morning of 11 December, to a background of continuing anti-Catholic unrest and violence in London and other cities. Catholic properties were burned and looted, Catholics themselves assaulted both verbally and physically. The embassies of European states known to be Catholic (France, Spain, Florence, Venice, Tuscany) were especially targeted.[14] Additional problems were created by Irish soldiery, demobilised though still armed, demoralised and often without the means of returning home, roaming the country and inviting unrest and violence. While most of them only wanted to get to the coast and take ship to Ireland, wild though usually unfounded rumours about their savage behaviour swept through towns and cities as distant from each other as Oxford and Wakefield, Yeovil and Bury St Edmunds.[15] The largely imaginary 'Irish Fright', as it came to be known, was for many people the defining aspect of those fraught December days.

Before leaving, James removed the Great Seal, symbol of royal authority, from the custody of its official guardian, the Lord Chancellor, and took it with him in a coach to the riverside. He was accompanied by Sir Edward Hales, a Catholic and formerly Governor of the Tower of London, and one or two other faithful friends and retainers. As they crossed over by boat to the opposite bank James leaned over the side and dropped the Seal into the Thames, from whose murky waters it was recovered by chance several months later by a fisherman.[16] His furtive journey then continued through rural Kent to Sheerness, where the party boarded a small sailing ship which, it was intended, would take them to France.

It was here – or perhaps at nearby Faversham, reports differ – that they ran out of luck. The ship needed to take on ballast before she could leave. During this process a band of seamen, zealously hunting for suspect Catholics, arrived on board and recognised Sir Edward as a local bigwig. He and his party were immediately taken into custody. Sir Edward was accompanied by an ill-dressed, 'ugly, lean-jawed, hatchet-faced popish dog' wearing a crucifix, who was assumed to be a Jesuit and rudely strip-searched for valuables. Not until the captives were carted off to the Queen's Arms tavern in Faversham for further interrogation was the true identity of this suspicious individual revealed. There are conflicting accounts as to what happened next. According to some, James was treated by the locals with surly insolence, and the money which had been taken from his purse (some 300 guineas) was not returned to him. However, the overwhelming body of evidence points to the money having been returned and having then been distributed by James amongst the townspeople.[17] But it is clear that his confinement was far from comfortable, and that this intensified the mood of depression which had already overtaken him.

Meanwhile in London, on learning the news of the king's defection, a hastily assembled committee of leading churchmen and noblemen met in Guildhall on the morning of 11 December to discuss the situation. An official Declaration was drawn up, in the names of 'the Lords Spiritual and Temporal ... pledging their support to the Prince of Orange in his endeavour to establish a free Parliament'. It received twenty-seven signatures. On the following day the committee published a further Proclamation, enjoining the public 'to keep the peace and forbear pulling down or defacing houses or buildings, especially those of foreign Ministers', and ordering sheriffs and JPs to use the militia 'to suppress riots which cannot be suppressed by the civil officers'.[18]

On 13 December news finally reached London of the king's plight at Faversham. The committee met, and dispatched Lord Winchilsea on a rescue mission to Kent. A letter was then sent to Prince William informing him of the situation. 'We think it our duty to acquaint your Highness that upon information brought to us this day that his Majesty is at Feversham [sic] ... we have ordered four Lords to attend him ... and we thought it necessary at the same time to send six score of the Guards and fifty Grenadiers to attend his Majesty's person ... We hope this that we have done will have your Highness' approbation.'[19] On the contrary, it did not. In fact William – now at Windsor – was seriously displeased, and would much have preferred James to have vanished from the scene unnoticed. Over the next few days his forbodings were to seem fully justified.

Lord Winchilsea's large and powerful posse duly scooped up James from the uncouth clutches of his Faversham captors, and set off with him to London. However, to everybody's surprise, what had started out as a rescue mission became, on reaching the capital (16 December), something of a triumphal procession. As though by magic large crowds appeared on the streets and balconies, not to jeer but to cheer, as their rescued monarch passed along amongst them on his way to Whitehall. Bells rang out in celebratory peals, and as darkness fell the skies were lit up by the cheerful flames of bonfires. James could hardly believe his luck. It seemed to him, and indeed to those with him, that not only were his people in a forgiving mood, they were actually glad to have him back. However, it seems clear also that their welcome was less for their king personally than for a sense that the Catholic menace had been removed and that public order and stability would now be restored. As for James himself, many citizens still regarded him as their rightful and anointed ruler who had been led astray by the machinations of ill-intentioned ministers and advisors.

Undoubtedly the most universally detested of those ministers was the Lord Chancellor, George Jeffreys. So it was no surprise when, on 12 December, an angry mob nearly succeeded in lynching him as he was desperately trying to escape to France. Having decided that the time had now come to exchange the sinking ship of state for a real one, Jeffreys had disguised himself as a sailor before boarding a Newcastle collier moored at Wapping. But before the boat could leave he was recognised – allegedly by a lawyer whom he had once characteristically bullied and shouted down in court, an experience not easily forgotten – and violently assaulted by the crowd. Only the intervention of the militia saved him from being torn apart, and at his own request they lodged him for safety's sake in the Tower. Once there, he survived almost unnoticed for a few more months, but on 18 April of the following year he died in his cell without having been either charged or tried. He was 40 years old. The immediate cause of death was uncertain but seems to have been a combination of several elements, amongst which a life-long over-indulgence in brandy (perhaps leading to a fatal apoplexy) was probably an important factor. A macabre twist was given to the account of his arrest by a report that the shock of seeing the terrible Jeffreys in custody gave the Lord Mayor a fatal seizure.[20]

Despite the general rejoicing, not everybody was pleased to hear of James' return. Prince William in particular found the news disturbing and probably for a short time even wondered whether the tide of events, which had so far carried him along very satisfactorily, might now suddenly turn against him. Indeed, 'He was in such a surprise … as made him stand at a gaze in some doubt with himself what was next to be done.'[21] Even while James was still en route to London (at Rochester) and had sent the Earl of Feversham over to Windsor with an invitation to a meeting at St James's Palace, William clearly revealed his temporary state of jumpy uncertainty by ordering the earl's immediate arrest and detention.[22] His pretext was that Feversham had disbanded the army without permission, although in fact the earl had obeyed the instructions of the *ad hoc* Guildhall committee 'to give all manner of necessary orders, either by removing the Forces to distant quarters or by any other way his Lordship thought most fit, for the preventing [of] hostilities'.[23] William soon had the sense to rescind his order (at the request, it is said, of the Dowager Queen Catherine of Braganza, then living in Somerset House), but he declined James' invitation and instead implemented some significant changes of his own.[24]

At Whitehall and St James's Palace, as the evening of 17 December drew on, the king's guards – many of whom had already declared their support for William – found themselves taken off duty and replaced by three battalions of tough, battle-hardened Dutch troops. (The Anglo-Dutch Brigade, backed by regular Dutch soldiers, had already begun to assert control over the streets of London.) Oblivious to this development, James himself retired to bed as usual, only to be woken again around midnight with the news that three noblemen had arrived from Windsor with an important message from William. The visitors were the Marquis of Halifax, the Earl of Shrewsbury and Lord Delamere, and their message, which they insisted on delivering without delay regardless of the late hour, was blunt and uncompromising. In order to avoid any further public disturbances, William required his father-in-law to leave London by 10 a.m. that very day, and proposed that he should go to Ham House on the Thames near Richmond, the richly appointed but by now somewhat faded home of the widowed Duchess of Lauderdale.

William's message and the obvious signs that, despite James's rapturous reception by Londoners, it was he and not James who was now calling the shots, finally convinced James that the game was up, at least for the time being. However, he was not attracted to the idea of Ham House as a refuge. Back in the 1670s the house had been a byword for opulence in its up-to-the-minute furniture, fittings and interiors, and was the epicentre of a vibrant social circle presided over by the Lauderdales. Charles II himself had dined there in 1672. But since the death of the duke in 1682 conditions in the house had declined as the Duchess struggled with a mountain of debt and her own increasing ill-health. The prospect of staying there for any length of time was not pleasant, and James turned it down out of hand, declaring that 'Ham was a very ill winter house, and unfurnished' (which was not true).[25] Instead he made an alternative suggestion – he would return to Rochester. To this the messengers responded that they would have to get fresh instructions, but that they would return in the morning.

Shuttling back and forth throughout the night (William by now having reached Syon House, the Middlesex home of the Duke of Northumberland), they cannot have had much if any sleep. Nevertheless they were back again on the morning of 18 December as promised, and reported that William was content that his father-in-law should go to Rochester. In fact William had probably already recognised that this might be a move which could work to his advantage, as will be seen.

At mid-morning James and his party left Whitehall by barge, attended by other barges containing a number of Dutch soldiers as guards. Amongst the group of loyal supporters was James Fitzjames, Duke of Berwick-upon-Tweed and bastard son of James by Arabella Churchill, sister of the traitorous John. An unfavourable tide meant that by evening they had only got as far as Gravesend, where they were forced to spend the night. However, there were no further delays and they duly reached Rochester next day. Already there was a noticeably lax attitude to security, giving James food for thought. Could it be that his duplicitous nephew and son-in-law was actually encouraging him to escape unhindered? Over the next three days James pondered the situation and considered his options, finally concluding that there was in fact only one – he would have to quit the country. Calling together his remaining friends and advisors, he announced his intention of leaving for France immediately. It was already obvious that no difficulties would be placed in his way. William had welcomed the choice of Rochester, as being far enough away from London to avoid any kind of public demonstration, and giving easy access to the sea. Accordingly he had issued specific orders that should James try to escape (as William fervently hoped he would) he was not to be impeded in any way. James himself was unaware of these orders, but he knew a good opportunity when he saw one.

The house where he was lodging, and which afterwards came to be known as Abdication House, was in Rochester High Street, conveniently near the River Medway. His host was Sir Richard Head.[26] On 23 December it was found that the guards — some of whom, in particular the officers, were Catholics — had been mysteriously withdrawn, leaving the coast clear for James, his son, two loyal naval officers named as captains Travanion and Macdonnel, and a Mr Biddulph, one of his grooms of the bedchamber, to leave the house quietly and go down to the shore. Here they boarded a rowing boat and were taken downriver to the mouth of the Medway which they reached early on Christmas Eve. Another boat took them along the coast of the Isle of Sheppey to the mouth of the River Swale, where after delays and discomfort they finally transferred to a small yacht, the *Henrietta*, which was to take them to France.[27] The weather was bitterly cold with an east wind, for this was the period of the 'little Ice Age' and the winter of 1688/69 was one of the coldest of the entire cycle; in January 1689 the Thames froze over and a 'frost fair' was held on the ice. The tiny cramped cabin had only just enough room in it for James and his son, and the only food available was some bacon fried in a pan which had a hole in it.[28] Despite the adverse conditions the *Henrietta* completed the crossing safely and anchored near Calais early on Christmas morning, although in France it was already 5 January (NS). Soon James was joyfully reunited with his wife and son at St Germain-en-Laye, the palace which had been assigned to them by Louis XIV.

On the same day that James left London for the last time William entered it from the west in triumph. Once again cheering crowds lined the streets and celebratory bonfires blazed, perhaps illustrating as much the fickleness of the public and a general inclination to have a jolly good time when the opportunity arose, as respect for William himself and the expectation of a hopeful and stable future free from the menace of Catholicism. Whatever the general public mood, the news of the king's defection left the Lords Spiritual and Temporal in something of a vacuum and for a time uncertain of what the next move should be. Had James really gone, and could his departure be regarded as abdication? What now was the position of William and his wife — should they simply be offered the Crown outright? How was Parliament to be summoned, since only the reigning monarch had the authority to call elections? On 23 December William, perplexed by the different Tory and Whig factions but determined to achieve his ultimate goal of sovereignty, issued an order desiring 'all such persons as have served … in any of the Parliaments that were held during the Reign of the late King Charles the Second, to meet us at St. James's upon Wednesday the sixth-and-twentieth of this Instant December' (although in fact they did not actually meet him until the 27 December).[29]

At the meeting these former MPs agreed on an address to William which began with a sycophantic preamble conveying their 'most humble and hearty thanks, for your coming into this kingdom, exposing your person to so great hazards, for the preservation of our religion, laws and liberties, and rescuing us from the miseries of popery and slavery'. In fact William himself had a quite different agenda which took more account of European politics than of England's religious differences, but the MPs were not to know that, although some might have had their suspicions. The address went on to ask William to take upon himself 'the Administration of publick Affairs, both Civil and Military, and the disposal of the publick Revenue'. In a moment of rare prescience it further asked him 'to take into your particular Care the present Condition of Ireland, and endeavour … to prevent the Dangers threatening that Kingdom'.

William was also asked that he should 'cause letters to be written containing directions for the election of Members of Parliament'.[30] This would be a Convention Parliament – that is, one not summoned by the sovereign. In a letter dated 29 December William signified his consent to this request and set the date of 22 January for the meeting of the Convention. He had already taken the reins of Government into his own hands on 28 December. On the same day the half-forgotten Titus Oates received a late Christmas present; he was released from prison and his pension was restored. He even got an interview with William.

The elections to the Convention Parliament were comparatively low-key, and both Houses duly met on 22 January 1689. This time the composition of the Commons achieved a reasonable balance between Whigs and Tories, unlike the recent previous parliaments which had been heavily weighted towards one side or the other. Nevertheless the Whigs had the edge. An intense debate immediately began in both Houses as to what form the monarchy should now take. It was generally accepted that James' days as king were over, although there was considerable argument as to whether he had actually abdicated or merely 'vacated' the throne. What was less certain was the identity of his successor. Nobody gave serious thought to the infant Prince of Wales, James' rightful son and heir. Initially the Whigs were for handing the crown outright to William and so bypassing the legitimate claims of his wife Mary. However, the mainly Tory Lords disagreed; a considerable body, led by Lord Danby, favoured Mary, with William as consort (a role which one day would be filled by Prince Albert).

On 31 January William conveyed to a private meeting of peers his reluctance to fill the role of 'gentleman usher to his wife'.[31] He looked on with increasing irritation as both Houses continued to debate the pros and cons of the situation in tedious detail. They were urged on by public debate conducted in a deluge of pamphlets, as well as by lively and sometimes heated discussion and argument often fuelled by alcohol, in streets, taverns, coffee houses and private homes. A petition said to show some 15,000 signatures, and asking that William and Mary should be invited to rule jointly, was suppressed by the authorities with the approval of William, who did not want to be associated with any kind of apparent populist influence.[32]

By the beginning of February William's patience, which had been rapidly wearing thin, was finally exhausted. So far he had kept his counsel. 'During these debates ... he stayed at St. James's, went little abroad, saw few people, heard all that was said, answered nothing, neither affected to be affable or popular, nor took any pains to gain over one person to his party.'[33] Already on 28 January John Evelyn had noted the 'morose temper of the Pr. of Orange, who shewed so little countenance to the noblemen & others [who] were expecting a more gracious and respectfull reception when they made their court'. Eventually the grumpy William again let it be known that, so far as he was concerned, acting as consort and so playing second fiddle to his wife was a non-starter. Nor would he act as regent – another idea put forward by the Lords. Furthermore, if the decision of the Convention was not favourable to him, he would quit England for good and take his army with him.[34] This threat caused some consternation amongst the politicians. Suppose a vengeful James, backed by powerful French forces, should return to reclaim the throne? And before that happened there could be further public disorder on a scale even worse than before. Another important factor in the debate was a message from the Princess Mary who was about to embark for England, to the effect that she had no intention of upstaging her husband, to whom she would always remain loyal. Her sister Anne similarly pledged her loyalty to both William and Mary.

In the face of these powerful obstacles the Convention had little room for further manoeuvre. By 6 February both Houses had agreed that the throne was indeed vacant, not merely temporarily abandoned. And so at the Whitehall Banqueting House on 13 February, after some more last-ditch argument, William and Mary were together received in state and finally and publicly proclaimed joint monarchs 'with wonderful acclamation & general reception, bonfires, bells, guns &c,' as noted by Evelyn (22 February). Similar demonstrations took place throughout the country, though it seems that not all were spontaneous and some were actively hostile.[35] In his acceptance speech William (clearly taking his cue from the 26 December address) claimed that, 'As I had no other intention in coming hither than to preserve your religion, laws and liberties, so you may be sure that I shall endeavour to support them.'[36] Naturally enough he made no reference to another intention which had weighed even more heavily with him throughout the entire campaign. This was, to make sure that England remained under his control rather than that of the French, and that he would be able to make legitimate use of the English army in defending his native country against them.

PALACES FIT FOR A KING

In 1689 William and Mary took up their official residence as joint monarchs in the old palace of Whitehall. But they had already decided that living there more or less full-time would not suit either of them. William found both the riverside location and the smoke-filled London atmosphere bad for his asthma, and Mary found the palace's sprawling buildings outdated, oppressive and inconvenient. Somewhere else would have to be found, on a healthier site but still within reach of London. The Tudor palace of Hampton Court, though certainly old-fashioned, was in reasonable repair, and they decided that it would offer the best solution. So they sent for the official architect, the Surveyor-General of the King's Works, Sir Christopher Wren, and asked him to carry out an update.

At the time of the Revolution Wren's principal ongoing project was also his life's greatest work – the building of the new cathedral of St Paul, a modern replacement for the old medieval cathedral of the same name which had been destroyed in the 1666 Great Fire of London. The foundation stone had been laid in June 1675, the start of a process that would not be completed until thirty-five years later in 1710. Thus the new St Paul's was nearing the half-way stage when William and Mary were crowned. The commission to re-shape Hampton Court (hopefully as a powerful rival to Versailles) was a chance for Wren to show that he was just as at home in designing large secular buildings as he was in producing ecclesiastical ones.

But the original conception was too grand, too expensive, and in the end only the south and east blocks were completed. Today the most striking feature is the long east front, imposing yet human in scale, with its measured sequence of stately windows punctuated by a pillared central block. Behind the first-floor windows stretches out the long parade of panelled state rooms, whilst the inner side of the block becomes the delightful Fountain Court with its arcaded ground floor and a striking third-storey line of circular windows wreathed in garlands of stone.

Despite the royal enthusiasm for Hampton Court as the ideal location, MPs were worried that the Palace was too far from London for there to be swift access to the king if necessary, especially during the winter.

There was also anxiety about the length of time it would take to complete Hampton Court. A compromise was found in the form of a small country house of about 1600 belonging to the Earl of Nottingham, in the village of Kensington. Purchased, with its estate, from the earl in June 1689 for £14,000, the house was handed over to Wren with instructions to modernise it and make it habitable as soon as possible. Today its most familiar aspect is the main three-storey south front, the tall elegant windows echoing those at Hampton Court, the centre emphasised by four ornamental pilasters (flat pillars). Wren's use of brick as the chief building material at both palaces (though Kensington did not become a palace officially until the eighteenth century) echoed contemporary Dutch taste and so ensured that the king would feel at home. This is especially true of Kensington; despite its dignified appearance, it too has about it a homely atmosphere which, together with the brick walls, would have reminded William of his Dutch palace of Het Loo.

The magnificent King's Gallery lies behind the main facade, and is the focal point of the two suites of interconnected state rooms designed for William and Mary respectively. The queen's rooms are still largely unaltered, although the king's underwent some changes during the eighteenth century, notably the addition of painted wall and ceiling decorations by William Kent. Work proceeded quickly and was sufficiently far ahead for the royal couple to move in on Christmas Eve 1689. They both got on well with Wren. When things went wrong at Hampton Court, involving some structural damage, William went out of his way to praise the designs. He also brushed aside criticism of the Fountain Court – the arcades, it was alleged, were too low – by saying that the work had been done 'according to his express orders'.

But it was Mary with whom Wren struck up the greatest rapport. Spirited and intelligent (Burnet says that she 'read much, both in history and divinity'), she also had a wide knowledge of scientific and artistic matters, and so could talk knowledgeably with the Surveyor about subjects of mutual interest to them both. During William's absence in Ireland she took a keen interest in the ongoing work at Hampton Court, so much so that Wren converted a small Tudor riverside building into temporary lodgings for her. She also approved the artists and craftsmen engaged by Wren to decorate his work and appreciated their contributions to it. These included the great woodcarver Grinling Gibbons ('discovered' by John Evelyn in 1671), and the French Huguenot ironmaster Jean Tijou. Gibbons' wonderful cascades of birds, fruit, flowers, foliage, drapery, musical instruments and many other creatures and objects, all fashioned from wood (often limewood, his favourite), seem to appear in every corner of Hampton Court and Kensington. The work of Tijou may be less generally well-known but is no less widespread. His delicate iron balustrades complement the grand staircases, and his glorious, feather-light screen – can it really be metal? – closes the vista at the end of the Hampton Court Privy Garden, overlooking the Thames.

Wren's friendship with Queen Mary was of sadly short duration, a mere five years, and her death in December 1694 was a personal blow. Ever a practical man, he expressed his grief in designing both her funeral carriage and the ceremonial platform on which her body lay in state in Westminster Abbey.

The official invitation to the new king and queen was actually enshrined in a Declaration of Rights, whose final draft the Convention had approved on 12 February, after the details had been mulled over for several days previously.[37] Much of this important document was later enshrined in a Bill of Rights (December 1689), and although it lacked the necessary teeth to enforce some of its clauses it has nevertheless long been regarded by many as being one of the fundamental building-blocks of the English Constitution. The first part began with a rousing denunciation of 'the late King James the Second, [who] by the assistance of divers evil counsellors, judges and ministers ... did endeavour to subvert and extirpate the Protestant religion and the laws and liberties of this kingdom'. It went on to list the various means by which James had tried to carry out his nefarious plan, including the perennial sore points of the dispensing powers, the setting up of the Ecclesiastical Commission, the 'raising and keeping [of] a standing army within this kingdom in time of peace without consent of Parliament', the tampering with the electoral process, and the corruption of the judicial system.

The second part of the Declaration set out ways of righting these wrongs, mainly by simply reversing them, but also by asserting the supremacy of Parliament over the monarchy. The MPs firmly stated their belief 'that election of members of Parliament ought to be free', and furthermore, that the freedom of speech and debates or proceedings in Parliament 'ought not to be impeached or questioned in any court or place out of Parliament'. With painful memories of the past, they also said that parliaments should be held more often, and that taxation without Parliamentary approval was illegal. They welcomed the help of 'his Highness the Prince of Orange, whom it hath pleased Almighty God to make the glorious instrument of delivering this kingdom from popery and arbitrary power', in setting up the Convention. The succession was firmly settled on Princess Anne and her descendants. To the final resolution 'that William and Mary, Prince and Princess of Orange ... be declared King and Queen of England, France and Ireland and the dominions thereunto belonging' was added the proviso that 'the sole and full exercise of the regal power be only in and executed by the said Prince of Orange in the names of the said Prince and Princess during their joint lives'. There was to be no future argument as to which of the dual monarchs really held the reins of power.

The Declaration ended with the following short oath of loyalty to the new king and queen, approved by both Houses and designed to replace all previous oaths: 'I, A. B., do sincerely promise and swear that I will be faithful and bear true allegiance to their Majesties King William and Queen Mary. So help me God.' Simple enough, it might be thought. Yet the requirement of all clergy and public servants to swear to this oath was to be the cause of huge problems for a great many people. Meanwhile preparations went ahead for the coronation which was fixed for 11 April.

Princess Mary had arrived from the Netherlands on 12 February, on the eve of her public acclamation as queen. At the ceremony itself many had expected her to apologise on behalf of her father, that things should have come to such a pass under his rule; it was also expected that she would have 'shewed some seeming reluctancy, at least, of assuming her father's crown', as Evelyn put it. On the contrary, she arrived at Whitehall apparently in high spirits, 'as to a wedding, riant & jolly, so as seeming to be quite transported' (*Diary*, 22 February). The following morning she rose early and, still in her nightdress, skipped gaily from room to room of the palace, chattering endlessly and giggling like a schoolgirl, while staff and courtiers looked on disapprovingly. Amongst them was Sarah, the wife of John Churchill and future Duchess of Marlborough, whose report was more down-to-earth and dramatic than that of John Evelyn. Mary, she said, ran about the palace 'looking into every closet and conveniency, and turning up the quilts upon the bed, as people do when they come into an inn ... which ... I thought very strange and unbecoming'.[38]

Such hoydenish behaviour did not go down well and was in strong contrast to that of her husband who (wrote Evelyn) 'has a thoughtful countenance, is wonderful serious & silent, [and] seems to treat all persons alike gravely'. However, all was not what it seemed. In fact William had given his wife strict instructions to put a cheerful face on things and not to appear downcast at the fate of her father. In obeying his wishes Mary had overdone the acting – indeed, she seems to have hammed it up rather more than he had intended, to the extent that she was now criticised for showing insufficient sympathy for her father's plight. It was not a good start. Nevertheless, once things had settled down, those around her came to appreciate her good humour and naturally lively personality which provided a welcome foil to her dour husband. One of her greatest fans was Bishop Burnet, who wrote that 'The Princess possessed all that conversed with her with admiration. Her person was majestic, and created respect; she had great knowledge, with a true judgement and a noble expression; a sweetness there was in her deportment that charmed, an exactness in her piety and virtue, a frugality in her expenses, an extensiveness in her charities, and a peculiar grace in bestowing them, so as to make her a pattern to all who saw her.'[39] Allowing, as always, for the bishop's partisan attitude, it does seem as though most of those who knew her were of much the same opinion.

Later, once William began to spend more time out of the country campaigning, he was able to leave the affairs of state in Mary's hands, for she showed herself to be a shrewd and capable ruler who was careful to remain apolitical at all times – in fact, the ideal constitutional monarch, just as had been envisaged in the Declaration of Rights.

The coronation took place as planned on 11 April. Much of the time-honoured ritual remained unchanged, but the all-important coronation oath was altered to take account of changed circumstances and was taken by each of the joint sovereigns. Both now promised to uphold the laws as agreed by Parliament, and to respect and support the reformed Protestant faith. Neither seems to have enjoyed the service much, William muttering that it was all a bit too 'popish' for his Calvanistic liking and Mary finding it all too over-the-top for hers. William, like James before him, received the crown, sceptres and orb originally made for Charles II in 1661. Mary wore her stepmother's crown but was given a new sceptre and orb, both of which (together with William's regalia) still form part of the Crown Jewels in the Tower of London.[40] The service itself differed in one important detail. Centuries of tradition had dictated that the crown should be placed on the monarch's head by the Archbishop of Canterbury. However, William and Mary were not crowned by William Sancroft but by Henry Compton, the ubiquitous Bishop of London, who also presided over the service. What had happened?

The fact was that after much soul-searching the archbishop had found that his conscience would not allow him to take the new oath of allegiance that was now required by Parliament. While he had fought King James every step of the way over the issue of Catholicism versus the Anglican Church, and had suffered public humiliation en route, this had not altered his sworn loyalty to the monarchy and the rightful succession. Some pragmatic Tories were prepared to swallow their misgivings and to accept William and Mary as monarchs *de facto*, if not *de jure* (in fact, if not by right). To Sancroft this was simply unacceptable. When his chaplain prayed for the new king and queen in the chapel at Lambeth Palace, he received a stern telling-off from the archbishop, who told him that 'he must either desist from praying for William and Mary or cease to officiate in the chapel; for as long as King James was alive, no other persons could be sovereigns of the country'.[41] There were many others who thought as he did, and one of these was Queen Mary of Modena's Attorney-General, Roger North.

Back in early January North had already set out his thoughts on the current political situation in a manuscript treatise entitled *The Present State of the English Government Considered*.[42] In this he had placed himself firmly in the ranks of those to whom even the *de facto* argument was flawed. 'How can he, who hath sworn that King James II is the only lawful king of this realm, or that he will bear faith and true allegiance to him, his heirs and successors, take those oaths to a usurper?', he asked rhetorically. To him the doctrine of the Divine Right of Kings, the cause of so much bloodshed earlier in his own century, was written in tablets of stone. These words reflected Sancroft's own beliefs so accurately that he was long thought to have been the author of the treatise. As William and Mary embarked together on their new reign it became clear that painful decisions would have to be made, consciences rigorously searched and lives disturbed before they could be sure how things stood between them and the people of England.

KILLIECRANKIE, GLENCOE AND THE BOYNE

word that came into frequent use during the years 1689 and '90 was 'nonjuror', meaning a person who refuses to take an oath – in this case, the oath of allegiance to William and Mary. Amongst the earliest of the nonjurors was Samuel Pepys, who resigned his post as Secretary to the Navy a week after the proclamation ceremony in the Banqueting House. To some extent this was because he could see that the old order was changing and he wanted no part of the inevitable upheaval. But chiefly it was because, although no believer in the Divine Right of Kings to rule without the sanction of Parliament, his personal loyalty to James II, whom he had known and served for many years and whose will, with others, he had witnessed, was simply not negotiable.[1] He handed over his files and papers without demur, but when ordered to leave his house on the grounds that it had also been used as his office, he not only refused but dug his heels in to such effect that the authorities gave up and allowed him to stay on unmolested.[2]

Such stubborn determination was characteristic of several high-profile nonjurors. One of the most outstanding, because of his position, was Archbishop Sancroft. The reason for his failure to officiate at the coronation had been duly noted, but no action was taken against him until 1 August. On that day he was officially suspended from office for six months – the statutory period allotted by Parliament to nonjurors, to give them time for reflection. When this period of grace failed to bring about any change in the archbishop's attitude, he was officially deprived of his office on 1 February 1690. At the same time four of the six bishops who had faced trial with him also lost their sees, and for the same reason – all were nonjurors. However, deprivation made no immediate difference to Sancroft; he continued to live at Lambeth Palace as though nothing had happened, and the authorities had to resort to legal action to evict him. Modern-day protesters who employ such delaying tactics might be surprised to learn that there is nothing new in their activities. The archbishop's dogged resistance surely contradicts Gilbert Burnet's assessment of him as 'a poor-spirited and fearful man'. He finally left Lambeth on 23 June 1691, 'poor as when he first entered it, taking nothing with him but his staff and his books'. He retired to his birthplace, Fressingfield in Suffolk, where he lived quietly and humbly until his death on 24 November 1693.[3]

Throughout this difficult period Roger North, as Sancroft's steward, had been at his side, to advise on the legalities of the situation and to give support. By now himself a convinced nonjuror, he also helped the other bishops with their individual problems, as well as lesser clergy. He continued to act as steward to the see of Canterbury, maintaining that his appointment was for life and that there were no legal grounds on which he could be removed, and he also refused to present himself to Sancroft's replacement John Tillotson, formerly Dean of St Paul's, a mild and humble man who had accepted his unlooked-for elevation with the greatest reluctance. Roger, as ever the astute lawyer, suspected a trap: 'It was expected that I should … wait on his pretended Grace to compliment him on his promotion, and so have put myself in a way to be wheedled and wire-drawn into an oath.'[4] Six months later his failure to take the all-important oath resulted in the inevitable official letter ordering him to resign the stewardship. He remained defiant but to no avail; finally and reluctantly clearing his desk (though hanging on illegally to original deeds and memoranda), he retired into rural obscurity in Norfolk.

Stories such as these illustrate the problems which faced nonjurors in England as they tried to come to terms with their changed circumstances. It has to be said that they were in a minority and represented only a small proportion of the population. In the Anglican Church, some 400 incumbents out of a possible 12,000 were forced to leave their parishes.[5] The more extreme nonjurors left the country for France, many of them to devote their time to fruitless plotting and, more enduringly, to earn the name of Jacobites (deriving directly from the Latin *Jacobus Rex*). But the majority of nonjurors simply kept their heads down and got on with their lives, despite the penalties they suffered, the disadvantages they endured, and the prejudices with which they were regularly confronted.

The momentous events of 1688–89 are often thought of purely in English terms. While the English connection is paramount, it is all too easy to forget that both Scotland and Ireland were also involved in the general upheaval. However, William did not forget. In October 1688, whilst still in The Hague and penning the *Declaration* in which he justified his reasons for invading England, he supplemented it with another similar document specifically addressed to the Scots. Kept informed by a coterie of exiled Scotsmen and by a network of spies in Scotland itself, he was well aware that across the border too there was much to be done. Though he was not particularly interested in Scotland or its politics he wanted the situation there to be stabilised, so that he would not need to be deflected from his main purpose, which was to keep Louis XIV at bay on the European mainland.

Whilst still on the throne King James had pursued broadly the same policies in Scotland as he had done in England – rigging the composition of the Scottish Parliament, introducing a creeping Catholicism into public appointments, ordering the suppression of any signs of Dissent including anti-Catholic preaching in the churches. The population reacted with violence and riots broke out in Edinburgh and Glasgow just as in London. Furthermore, James' efforts to follow his much-vaunted English policy of offering toleration to minority faiths, in the hopes of gaining their support, foundered on the adamantine rock of Scottish Presbyterianism.

Since 1582 there had been in fact two parallel Churches in Scotland. In that year the original Church of Scotland, ripe for reformation and fired by the Calvinistic preaching of the redoubtable John Knox (whose influence, despite his death in 1572, remained undiminished), officially re-shaped its theology. Crucially, it rejected governance by bishops in favour of genuine Presbyterian control by elders. Such church members and clergy as remained faithful to the old-established beliefs now formed themselves into the Scottish Episcopal Church, whose title reflected its continuing allegiance to the bishops. James I, Charles I and Charles II had all tried through different methods to bring the Church of Scotland back under episcopal control, but had signally failed to do so. Thus the established Church of Scotland itself represented the main anti-Catholic voice of opposition to King James, in a way that the disparate groups of Non-conformists and Dissenters in England had never done, and its united voice was far more powerful than theirs had ever been. There was no way that Presbyterians were going to form an alliance with Catholics on Scottish town councils and similar public bodies, as Quakers and other dissenting sects had done in England.

The final months of James' reign in Scotland passed in an uneasy peace, but public fears about his political intentions were once again aroused when news reached the Scottish cities of the birth of the Prince of Wales. It was received with a marked and ominous lack of enthusiasm. Yet there were no immediate repercussions, and James was lulled into a dangerously false sense of security. Thus, when eventually he needed troops to confront William's invading army, he had no hesitation in withdrawing the bulk of his Scottish forces and dispatching them south to Carlisle. This was a serious mistake. Whilst a proportion of the population remained loyal, anti-Catholic rioting began in Edinburgh in December 1688 and spread throughout much of southern Scotland. Episcopalian clergy also became targets for Presbyterian mobs and in many cases were physically ejected from their livings.[6]

The arrival of William was broadly welcomed by the Scots, who looked to him – as did the English – to provide them with stable Government and to root out all forms of popery from their country. The only group who did not welcome him were the committed Jacobites, who remained loyal to James and to the Catholic faith, and who were domiciled mostly in the north of Scotland, especially the Highlands. In

London William was badgered by both the Presbyterian and Episcopalian factions, each pleading their case. The Presbyterians sought full recognition of their Church and an end to the indignities and suffering allegedly heaped upon them in previous reigns by the Episcopalians. For their part, the Episcopalians wanted a guarantee of security for the bishops in their sees, although the bishops themselves were keen to stress their sworn and continuing loyalty to James. Clearly it would be desirable to reach a compromise of some kind, but this could not be achieved without reasoned discussion and debate. Accordingly William was persuaded to summon a Scottish Convention, which would examine not only the religious differences but also the whole question of the succession and the position of William and Mary themselves.

On 14 March 1689 the Convention met in Edinburgh under the presidency of the Duke of Hamilton (a committed Presbyterian), and was in session for a month. At the end of that time and after a great deal of constructive argument it drew up a document called the Claim of Right, in parallel with the English Declaration of Rights, although the Scottish version was more focussed and forthright. In this document the Convention declared that James VII of Scotland had not only vacated the throne ('forfaulted' was the actual legal term used) but had not even been legally entitled to occupy it, since he had not taken the coronation oath.[7] Many of the accusations levelled at James were the same as those produced in England – keeping a standing army, tampering with the justice system, levying illegal taxes etc. – but there was even more emphasis on the damage done by his pro-Catholic policies. Ominously, the Presbyterian faction in the Convention took advantage of this and used the Claim to attack episcopacy in general.[8]

Having therefore agreed almost unanimously that James was now a royal *persona non grata* the Convention turned its attention to his successors and was not long in deciding that the Scottish Crown should be offered jointly to William and Mary. On 11 April proclamation of their accession was duly made in Edinburgh and the other major cities in Scotland. However, an important two-fold condition of the offer was that they should accept both the Claim of Right and the Scottish coronation oath, specifically in that order (though no such stipulations had been made in England).[9] A small deputation of three travelled to London to present these conditions, to which William agreed, and on 11 May the Banqueting House was once again the setting for a ceremony at which the joint sovereigns were invested with authority to reign, with William again having the executive power. Yet ultimately they were no more above the law than in England, as the fall of James had so recently illustrated, and both the Scottish Claim and the English Declaration had made it clear that in the last resort the monarch was answerable to the people.

On the following 5 June the Convention metamorphosed itself into a Parliament and began to pass measures which dealt with the points raised in the Claim of Right. Unlike the two Houses of the English Parliament, the Scottish version – dating back to the thirteenth century – was composed of representatives of the Three Estates (in old Scots, the *Thrie Estaitis*), these being bishops, then lairds (nobles of different ranks), then burgesses. Again unlike England, all the members sat together in a single chamber. With the bishops gone, the Estates had then to be re-formed, and the three divisions now consisted of (1) nobility, (2) barons and laymen representing the shires, and (3) burgesses. The newly constituted Parliament of 1689 not only had no place for the bishops, but on 22 July pressed home the demands of the Claim of Right by abruptly abolishing episcopacy altogether. Then in the spring and early summer months of 1690 the Parliament followed up its new advantage with a number of significant measures. Notable amongst them was one reinstating those Presbyterian ministers who had been dispossessed since the Restoration, and another confirming the system of Presbyterian government within the now established Church of Scotland (known generally as the Kirk).

In this sudden reversal of their fortunes many Episcopalian clergy suffered grievously. Not only were they turned out of their parishes to make way for Presbyterian ministers, but they also found themselves – like their English counterparts – unable to swear the oath of allegiance to William and Mary which became now, as in England, an inescapable duty required of all those holding any kind of public office, whether in Church or State. However, they chose on the whole to suffer in silence and did not actively join the cause of those most vociferously opposed to the new regime – the Jacobites. This movement, whose *raison d'être* was its loyalty to King James and his heirs, was the first to mount any kind of serious challenge to the authorities – a challenge led by the handsome, valiant and charismatic John Graham (b. 1648), Laird of Claverhouse, 1st Viscount Dundee and the 'Bonny Dundee' of folk-song and legend.

Ironically, as a young Cavalry officer serving in the Netherlands, John Graham had gone to the aid of Prince William of Orange in battle, and had been duly commended and promoted. He was only two years older than William. On returning to England he was sent up to southern Scotland by Charles II with orders to disrupt the seditious assemblies of the Covenanters. This he did with such violent enthusiasm that he became known in that area as 'Bluidy Clavers', in strong contrast to his alter ego as Bonnie Dundee. However, the Covenanters struck back, and on 1 June 1679 at the Battle of Drumclog, Claverhouse (as he was then generally known) was ignominiously forced to flee. Help soon arrived in the person of the Duke of Monmouth at the head of significant reinforcements and with orders to take command of the situation. At the ensuing Battle of Bothwell Brig (22 June) the tables were turned and the Covenanters routed, a defeat to which Claverhouse and his dragoons – all thirsting for revenge – made a decisive and bloody contribution. Criticised for some of his more extreme actions, he responded with a chilling self-justification which has become all too familiar in recent times through its use by all kinds of dubious military and paramilitary characters: 'In any service I have been in I never inquired farther in the laws than the orders of my superior officers.'[10]

In Government circles in London, Claverhouse was now in high favour and he climbed rapidly up the social and military ladders. In 1683 he was appointed to the Scottish Privy Council and in 1686 rose to the rank of major-general. In the same year he became Lord Provost of the city of Dundee, of which he had already been Constable since 1684. Thus began a love-hate relationship between himself and the citizens of Dundee, who were later to show a deep-seated mistrust of their provost. In 1688 Claverhouse returned to England with the Scottish forces ordered south by King James, who on this occasion created him Viscount Dundee. The city, it seems, remained unimpressed by this honour. When the anti-Dutch campaign petered out the new Viscount, by now a steadfastly loyal supporter of James, returned to Scotland, hoping to have some influence on the Jacobite side in the Convention.

It took only four days of attendance at the Convention to show Dundee that he and his associates were supporting a lost cause, and he left Edinburgh on 18 March with a body of loyal troopers. He then raised the standard of active rebellion on the mound known as Dundee Law (actually an extinct volcano), which although now in central Dundee was at that time outside the walls – for in an act of sullen defiance the citizens had closed the gates against him. Dundee now attempted to raise an army from amongst the clans, and although he failed to gain the support of many of the powerful anti-Catholic Scottish leaders he did succeed in amassing some 2,000 men. At the same time it must be admitted that the Highlanders' first loyalty was always to their chieftain rather than to a particular cause. For example, a strong incentive for the otherwise disparate clansmen to unite in a common objective on this occasion was undoubtedly their deep hatred for the clan Campbell whose chieftain, the Earl of Argyll, had declared himself on the side of William and Mary.

From his refuge at St Germain King James had issued a proclamation which endorsed Dundee's actions and commanded all loyal Scots to join the cause.[11] For some weeks Dundee waited for a sign that James himself would appear on the scene, backed by Irish and possibly French reinforcements. Nothing happened – James was too busy himself in Ireland. Meanwhile a Government army twice the size of Dundee's and under the command of the able if somewhat stolid General Hugh Mackay had been sent to put down the rebellion. The two opposing forces met to do battle at the brooding and rugged Pass of Killiecrankie near Pitlochry, and given the disparity in their numbers the outcome seemed to be in little doubt. However, what the clansmen lacked in manpower they made up for in enthusiasm. They charged the ranks of Government soldiers with such ferocity that within a few minutes Mackay's men had fled and all was over. Ironically, their rapid defeat had been due partly to a purely technical problem. Faced with a swiftly oncoming horde of roaring and mostly barefooted Highlanders brandishing claymores (the famous 'Highland Charge'), the men had simply not enough time to fix their clumsy 'plug' bayonets into the mouths of their muskets, and so could not defend themselves at close quarters. Stung by his defeat, Mackay himself was later to invent a version of the ring bayonet which could be fixed round the musket barrel instead of being stuffed into it, so enabling firing to continue until the last moment.

Government losses were some 2,000 slaughtered 'redcoats', while the clans lost about half that number. Yet theirs was a hollow victory, for amongst the dying lay Bonnie Dundee himself, cut down by a musket ball as he led a cavalry charge. He was carried to Blair Castle, a few miles away, and three days later was buried in the crypt of St Bride, a small kirk (now ruined) in the grounds of the castle. His memorial is a nineteenth-century tablet in the crypt, and his breastplate survives in the castle. Three years later General Mackay was himself killed in action in Flanders.

With the death of Dundee any significant physical opposition to the new regime was effectively stifled in Scotland. Nevertheless contentious bickering between the Protestant and Episcopalian factions continued at a high level of intensity. The perception amongst the Episcopalians that they were gradually being pushed into a corner meant that many joined the Jacobite cause who might otherwise not have done so. In due time this situation contributed to the challenges with which the Government was to be confronted in 1715 and 1745. Those two famous though unsuccessful uprisings lie outside the scope of this book. However, we cannot ignore one other incident which took place in 1692, in circumstances so horrific that it is still widely remembered today. This was the infamous Massacre of Glencoe.

Despite the uneasy stand-off which had followed Killiecrankie, there were still enough pockets of resistance in the Highlands to give the authorities cause for concern. The continuing unrest was a drain on both the manpower and the finances of King William, at a time when he was about to undertake a new campaign in Europe.[12] And so in June 1691 a peace treaty was drawn up between the Government and the clans. Amongst other things this promised to cancel out their war record. In return their chieftains were required to swear the oath of loyalty to William and were given until 31 December to do it. All did so before the deadline – except one. This was Alastair MacIain of Glencoe. The glen itself was an inhospitable, frowning valley which was nevertheless home to a branch or 'sept' of the clan Macdonald, headed by the imposingly big, bearded MacIain.

In fact MacIain had technically been in time but by 31 December, due to the winter weather and his own unwise procrastination, had only reached Fort William where Colonel Hill, the governor, refused to accept his oath. The colonel said that he was not the appropriate official to witness the oath, and directed MacIain to the Sheriff of Argyll at Inverary, Sir Colin Campbell, at the same time giving MacIain a letter confirming his appearance on 31 December and willingness to swear. Owing to various delays, some due to the wintry travel conditions, others probably deliberately engineered by ill-wishers, several days then passed before MacIain was able to get to see Sir Colin and duly take the oath. The chief then returned to Glencoe, confident that all would now be well. However, he had reckoned without a coterie of devious and calculating enemies.

First amongst these was Sir John Dalrymple, the London-based Secretary of State for Scotland. Sir John, a Lowland Scot, despised the clan system and hated the Highlanders, who in his opinion needed to be taught a lesson in humility and subservience. MacIain's tardiness in subscribing to the oath of loyalty presented the perfect opportunity for such a lesson. A staunch Protestant, Sir John also loathed the Highlanders for their Catholicism. Supported in his designs by the two Campbell cousins John, Earl of Bredalbane and Holland, and Archibald, Earl (later Duke) of Argyll, he persuaded King William to sign an order for the virtual extermination of the clan in Glencoe. The officer charged with this horrendous responsibility was yet another Campbell – Captain Robert Campbell of Glenlyon, whose orders were 'to fall upon the rebels ... and put all to the sword under seventy'. There were to be no prisoners.

At the end of January 1692 the captain arrived in Glencoe with two companies of footguards numbering over 100 men, claiming that for the time being they were to be based in the glen. The soldiers were billeted on the clansmen who for two weeks showed them the hospitality for which Highlanders were renowned. Then, early on the morning of 13 February, at the height of a seasonal blizzard, the slaughter began. Men – and it seems even some women and children – were killed wholesale in their beds, in their homes, and on the mountainsides as they tried to flee. Their roughly built, turf-roofed cottages were torched over their heads whilst they were still inside, and as they ran out they were shot down or bayoneted. It is generally accepted that the number of clansmen murdered was thirty-eight including MacIain himself, but certainly others, and also many women and children, died from exposure to the elements.[13]

Yet the massacre was not the total success that Sir John Dalrymple had hoped and intended. A number of the soldiers involved found ways to avoid action, while others passed on hurried warnings to potential victims. Some of those victims did escape to tell the tale, and their harrowing reports were enough to blacken the name of Campbell for many years to come. Even more seriously for the Government, Jacobite resolve, which had been weakening, was given a major boost which was to carry it forward to the uprisings of the next century.

Opinions have varied over the years as to the extent of the king's personal complicity in the atrocity of Glencoe, but as usual the truth seems to lie somewhere in between. Much of what he knew about Scotland was what his advisors told him, and the Macdonalds of Glencoe were probably presented to him as little more than a band of thieving cattle-rustlers who deserved to be severely punished as an example to others. Moreover at the time his mind was chiefly on other things, especially on the situations in Ireland and in Europe, and against the backdrop of these designs the petty crimes of a few malcontents in the far-off Scottish Highlands cannot have carried much weight with him. On the other hand he did sign the order and so sanctioned the draconian solution to the problem. For this unthinking act he cannot avoid some censure. But even before it took place, the scandal of the Glencoe Massacre was overshadowed by events in Ireland so momentous that their echoes still reverberate loudly to this day.

During the reign of Charles II the situation in Ireland had been relatively stable, at least on the surface, with Protestants in the ascendancy in the Church and in most positions of authority. However, with the accession of James all this was to change. The Catholic population, both native Irish and 'Old English' (i.e. those whose families were not originally native to Ireland but had come over from England as settlers), welcomed the new order and looked forward to the restoration of their rights and, in many cases, the estates of which they had been originally deprived during the 1640s and '50s. The Protestants, on the other hand, prepared to resist all attempts to change the status quo, by force if necessary.

The shape of things to come was embodied in the form of Robert Talbot, a Catholic of English ancestry and a long-time friend of James, whose pre-1660 exile and subsequent return he had shared. Despite this friendship (which included covering up for James' many sexual intrigues), Talbot was himself implicated by Titus Oates in the Popish Plot (1678) and for a time had to retreat to France. In 1683, taking advantage of the improved political situation, he returned to Ireland and busied himself in plotting and planning to restore the lands and fortunes of the Old English Catholic community. When in 1685 his old friend the Duke of York succeeded to the English throne as James II, Talbot's hour had come at last.

It was not long before the new king was showing a gratifying trust in Talbot's abilities and judgement in relation to Irish affairs. Although James had installed the Earl of Clarendon as his Lord Lieutenant in Ireland it was clear that most of his advice was in fact coming from Robert Talbot.[14] This was underlined in June 1685 when Talbot was raised to the peerage as Earl of Tyrconnell, effectively becoming James' deputy in all but name. Lord Tyrconnell, as he had now become, was further appointed commander of the army in Ireland, a post which enabled him to pursue unhindered one of his primary objectives, which was to purge the army of all Protestants regardless of their abilities or record of service. As in England, further purges followed – of the Bar, of JPs and sheriffs, of civic bodies and corporations. In January 1687 Clarendon was recalled to London and was replaced by Tyrconnell who now became Lord Deputy, a move which further emboldened the Catholic community.

The impending Dutch invasion caused the king to demand troops from Ireland to help in the defence of England, and Tyrconnell provided a force of almost 3,000 men. However, he more than made up the deficit in Ireland by greatly increasing the size of the army there, until by

February 1689 the number of men at his disposal totalled not far short of 45,000.[15] It hardly mattered that the majority were rough country lads, ill-equipped, untrained and (to begin with) ill-disciplined – it was the sheer weight of numbers that impressed. Alarmed by these developments, the Protestant community – already increasingly harried and harassed by Catholic tactics, including the blatant arming of the civilian population – took fright. As their lands were seized and their livestock wantonly slaughtered around them, many fled the country altogether, making for the east coast mainland. Others sought the shelter of the traditional Protestant areas and strongholds in Ulster, in particular Derry (the Irish form of the Anglicised Londonderry) and Enniskillen, although other centres such as Dublin and Cork also resisted the persecutions for a while.

On 7 December 1688 a Catholic regiment appeared ominously outside the walls of Derry, ostensibly to replace the Protestant garrison. While the city fathers dithered over their reaction, in a famous historical episode which is still celebrated annually in the city a group of thirteen young apprentices zealously closed the city gates and occupied the arsenal. A few days later the citizens of Enniskillen followed their example. These and other acts of Protestant defiance convinced Tyrconnell that the time had come to make serious decisions, and he sent to King James in France assuring him of Irish support and urging him to return to reclaim his rightful authority. In fact Tyrconnell probably had little or no interest in helping James to regain the English and Scottish thrones; what he wanted was an independent Catholic kingdom of Ireland with James as its titular head – or, if not James himself, then perhaps one of James' sons.[16] Tyrconnell himself does not seem to have had ambitions to fill the post.

In addition to James and Tyrconnell, a powerful third party now became involved in the Irish decision-making process – James' host in France, Louis XIV. Left to himself, and after all the stresses and strains of the recent past, James would probably rather have chosen to continue his unaccustomed comfortable family life at St Germain. However, Louis had other ideas. The arrival of James in Ireland would be precisely the kind of distraction needed to occupy William in England and steer his attention away from Louis' activities in Europe.[17] It was therefore politely made clear to James that it was his sacred duty to go to Ireland and begin the process of reclaiming his birthright. It was also made clear that unfortunately no French troops would be available for the time being, but that French officers and advisors would be on hand to offer counsel and to monitor the progress of the exercise. There was a vague suggestion that if all went well French troops might perhaps follow at a later date.

On 12 March 1689 James and his party arrived on a French vessel (one of a small fleet) at Kinsale, where to the bracing sound of the bagpipes he was greeted with wild enthusiasm. By 14 March he was in Cork and being welcomed by his old friend Lord Tyrconnell. Their reunion could not alter the fact that, whereas Tyrconnell saw James as king of the Irish, to James Ireland was merely a staging-post in his reconquest of the mainland. Nevertheless he played his part with dignity and, once settled in Dublin Castle, called a session of the Irish Parliament for 7 May 1689. Meanwhile he and Tyrconnell had decided that their first aim must be the suppression of Protestant revolt, beginning with the unruly citizens of Derry. By the time the Parliamentary session had begun, the siege of Derry was well under way.

'To a military eye, the defences of Londonderry appeared contemptible,' wrote Macaulay, and he went on to explain why:

> The fortifications consisted of a simple wall overgrown with grass and weeds; there was no ditch even before the gates; the drawbridges had long been neglected … the parapets and towers were built after a fashion which might well move disciples of Vauban [the great French military engineer] to laughter; and these feeble defences were on almost every side commanded by heights.[18]

The governor of the city, Lieutenant-Colonel Robert Lundy, apparently believed that it was indefensible and that consequently defeat was certain. It was widely thought (and still is today) that his attitude was not down to cowardice but to treachery, and that he was at heart a supporter of King James.

Whatever the truth of these suspicions, it is perhaps significant that when on 14 April a small English fleet appeared in the bay with a total of two regiments on board, Lundy's advice to their commanding officer,

Colonel Cunningham, was so negative that the colonel decided to withdraw his forces without making any attempt to land. At the same time Lundy sent a covert message to enemy HQ guaranteeing that the city would capitulate peacefully. However, the citizens (their numbers now swelled many times by the influx of refugees) were made of sterner stuff than their governor. Incensed by his weak-kneed attitude and suspected treachery, they disowned his authority and took up arms, the able-bodied men forming themselves into a Protestant force of about 7,000 which was strongly supported by their womenfolk. What they lacked in military preparation and equipment they more than made up for in a spirit of courageous defiance, and in this spirit they awaited the arrival of James and Tyrconnell with the Catholic army.

On 18 April the army duly appeared before the walls of Derry and James himself rode forward to within 100 yards of the ramparts, fully expecting that his appearance in person would cow the rebels into immediate subjection. He received a nasty surprise when, instead of cries for mercy, robust shouts of 'No surrender!' were heard, accompanied by bursts of cannon fire, one of which killed an aide-de-camp who was riding at his side. The king abruptly left the scene and soon returned to the safety of Dublin, leaving the prosecution of the siege to the French General Maumont. In a series of courageous sallies over the next few weeks – during the first of which, on 21 April, Maumont himself was killed – the men of Derry managed to create havoc amongst their besiegers, but were forced eventually to retire behind their ramparts. In June the Catholic army – now led by the cautious Marshal Conrad von Rosen – made one further determined attempt to enter the city, but was repulsed by the defenders with severe losses. There was nothing for it but to resort to the tactics of blockade and starvation. A different dimension was now added to the sufferings of Derry.[19]

Meanwhile in Dublin the Irish Parliament finally met. Whereas formerly the composition of the Parliament had been fairly evenly balanced between the two main communities, now – thanks chiefly to Tyrconnell's manipulations – the Members were mainly Catholic, some Irish, the majority Old English. They approved legislation which confirmed James' undoubted right to the throne and condemned as totally unlawful any attempt to unseat him. Other laws were framed to promote liberty of conscience and (despite all that had gone before) the suppression of religious persecution, and to restore the rights of landowners to the status quo of the pre-1640s, in the process annulling the Act of Settlement of 1662 which had confirmed the Protestant ascendancy. As a corollary to this, and against James' wishes, the Parliament passed an Act of Attainder aimed specifically at a total of over 2,000 individual Protestants who were judged to have treasonably supported William of Orange.[20]

News of this measure reached London early in July. Accounts of the consequent flight to Ulster and England of many more Protestant refugees, and above all of the continuing sufferings of the emaciated yet still defiant people of Derry (who were now reduced to eating dogs, cats, rats and such few horses as remained), added to the sense of outrage, and there was popular demand for swift action. In the final days of July a relief force under General Percy Kirke finally broke through the boom which the besiegers had installed across the River Foyle, and the siege was lifted. It had lasted 105 days. The Catholic army, bruised, battered and ultimately unsuccessful in its primary aim, struck camp and retired from the scene, having lost an estimated 8,000 men (many from disease) as against a possible total of about 3,000 of the garrison in Derry.[21] At the same time Enniskillen too found freedom when its defenders, under officers sent by Kirke together with supplies of weapons and ammunition, took on an army sent to destroy them and routed it completely at Newtown Butler. The treacherous Lundy escaped the fury of the Derry citizens and fled to Scotland, but ended up in the Tower of London. Today he is still remembered in Ulster, though not for anything to his credit; his effigy, like that of Guy Fawkes, is annually cremated, and his name is synonymous with traitor.

For James in Dublin all this was bad news which very soon became even worse. In London emergency planning had continued, and as a result there arrived at Bangor (Ulster) on 13 August a substantial body of troops (around 17,000) headed by King William's aged commander-in-chief the Duke of Schomberg. Yet this army was ill-equipped to withstand the rigours of an Irish winter which, once begun, soon took its toll of men. By the end of its first six months in Ireland the army had lost over a third of its strength to sickness and disease, fostered by poor planning and malnutrition.[22] One report noted that the troops 'were so overrun with lice that vast numbers of them dyed [sic]'.[23]

James now began to entertain faint hopes that he might finally prevail, but in fact his own position was not much better. Although his army was already about twice the size of Schomberg's even before it had been further reinforced by several thousand troops from France (Louis XIV having at last decided to lend a hand), much of it was poorly armed and badly trained. It was clear that an impasse had been reached, and William was determined to end it. No longer in Ireland, any more than in Scotland, could he afford to tolerate the festering sores of a rebellion which served only to encourage the hopes of James, to say nothing of the more grandiose visions of Louis. He decided to assemble another army, properly prepared and victualled, and this time he would lead it himself. With a flash of wry humour, he told Bishop Burnet that 'going to a campaign was naturally no unpleasant thing to him; he was sure he understood that better than how to govern England'. Nevertheless it would be a wrench to leave his wife amid the peaceful surroundings of Hampton Court and its stately gardens, for whose improvement both sovereigns were together busy formulating plans. William had no personal animosity towards his father-in-law, and vetoed as treachery a plan to lure James onto a ship in Dublin and effectively kidnap him.[24]

GARDENS OF DELIGHT

When in 1660 King Charles II and his court returned from their Continental exile they trailed behind them a variety of trendy new fashions, mostly French in origin and affecting a wide field of taste in such things as clothing, furniture, painting, music – and gardens.

The English garden of Tudor times had in general been an inward-looking square enclosure, affording space for flowers, grass, arbours, trellis, fruit trees, fountains, statuary, sometimes even a maze. In particular the Tudor garden was noted for its arrangements of geometrically shaped beds, each containing a 'knot' or intricate pattern. These patterns were picked out either in low-growing plants such as dwarf box, rosemary or thrift, or in coloured gravels or brick-dust.

The Tudor garden was a typically scaled-down English interpretation of the Italian Renaissance garden, in which the horizons were wider, the water features larger, the emphasis on formal greenery and statuary more carefully considered. But it was in France that these features loomed largest and were most closely to influence garden development in England. Soon after 1660 Louis XIV's celebrated garden designer Andre Le Notre began work on the huge garden at Versailles.

Le Notre's visionary conception produced a garden of apparently limitless boundaries created by clever tricks of perspective. The plan was based on a central axial avenue from which radiated secondary paths, the whole forming a grid of mathematical proportions and precision. The hedged areas between the paths were filled with various attractions such as *bosquets* or groves of small trees, statuary, clipped greenery (topiary), *pavilions d'amour* and ornamental ponds. At the intersections of the various avenues and paths, fountains of all shapes and sizes provided dramatic punctuation points. But amongst the most spectacular features of the garden were the great *parterres* – ornamental beds related to the Tudor knot but much larger, their florid patterns and swirling arabesques laid out in turf, gravel, sand, spar (mineral chippings) or other materials. Unlike the self-contained knots, the parterres were an integral part of the whole garden design and were intended to be seen from first-floor height, for it was only from such a vantage point that their carpet-like patterns could be fully appreciated. These patterns were often based on those used for embroidery and so were called *broderies*.

Louis XIV was very proud of his great garden and liked nothing better than to tour round it in a special wheeled chair pushed by a gigantic guardsman. He wrote a guidebook to the garden and from it would point out the various beauty spots en route to the crowd of reluctant, foot-sore courtiers and visitors who plodded along behind him. Charles II was spared the tour, as he had left France before work on the Versailles garden had properly started, but he certainly got to know a lot about it and tried more than once to persuade Le Notre to visit England. The great man never came (though it seems he did send some plans), but nevertheless his influence was strongly felt, and today nowhere more so than at Hampton Court, in the area known now as the Great Fountain Garden.

This area lies on the east side of the palace and in 1662 was laid out in a well-established plan consisting of a series of straight lines radiating from a semi-circular base. Because of its shape this plan is generally known as the *patte d'oie* or goose-foot pattern. At Hampton Court the lines were composed of formal avenues of lime trees planted in double rows, except for the central avenue which took the form of a canal and was known as the Long Water. John Evelyn visited the garden on 9 June 1662 and found the work almost completed: 'the Park formerly a flat, naked piece of ground, now planted with sweet rows of lime trees, and the canal for water now near perfected.'

And so when William and Mary first arrived at Hampton Court they found that some of the basic elements of the fashionable Versailles-type garden were already in place. (Even the probable designer, Andre Mollet, was French.) But one important feature was missing – there were no parterres. Accordingly the semi-circular area was laid out with *broderie* parterres intersected by wide gravelled paths and punctuated by a series of twelve fountains, which now gave their name to the Court. Another, larger fountain in a huge basin formed the centrepiece. The outlines of the whole design may still be traced today.

As an antidote to all this grandeur, Queen Mary indulged her love of flowers, and an area near her temporary lodgings was set aside for them. She collected rare and exotic plants from distant countries, many of them kept from frost in early heated greenhouses or 'stoves'. Sadly she did not live to see completion of the next important development at Hampton Court, which was the Privy Garden on the south side of the palace. While William recognised the need to make a grand political statement with the Great Fountain Garden (as it was now called), he now also wanted something more personal, reminiscent of the garden at Het Loo, his hunting lodge back home in the Netherlands.

Because of the spatial constraints imposed by the grid-like pattern of Dutch canals, it was not possible in the Netherlands to achieve the sweeping vistas of the French garden, and so the borders of the Dutch garden tended to be more clearly defined. As a result, although laid out geometrically with fashionable parterres and associated features, many Dutch gardens of the period conveyed a sense of privacy, aided by the widespread use of hedging and greenery, especially topiary. So while the parterres of the Privy Garden were certainly grand, they were not as large or as imposing as those of the Great Fountain Garden. In addition the view across the River Thames at the bottom of the garden, instead of leading the eye into the distance in the French manner, was closed off by Jean Tijou's magnificent ironwork screen.

Tijou was a French Huguenot, and so was William's favourite designer Daniel Marot, who supplied patterns for many of the parterres. But much of the work on the Privy Garden was carried out by Henry Wise, who with his partner George London ran a highly successful nursery garden at Brompton near Kensington, on a site now partly occupied by the Science and Natural History museums. Wise and London also provided a Dutch-style garden for Kensington Palace. Today it is still possible to appreciate the work of these dedicated men at Hampton Court, for the Privy Garden was magnificently restored between 1992 and 1995. Yet none of their work would have been possible had it not been for the love of both William and Mary for their gardens.

William and his newly formed army arrived at Carrickfergus in mid-June 1690, and no doubt the old Duke of Schomberg was only too glad to hand over command. In contrast to James' raw Irish recruits, the majority of William's well-armed troops were seasoned veterans and the best of them were from the Netherlands and Denmark, backed up by a motley assortment of English, Scots, Irish Protestants, French Huguenots and Germans. Most authorities agree that William's forces – including those already present in Ireland under Schomberg – totalled about 36,000, although there is some confusion as to exactly how that number was made up.[25] They marched purposefully south towards Dublin and on 29 June reached the banks of the River Boyne, some 25–30 miles north of Dublin, to find that James had already set up camp on the other side of the river. Not far distant, near the mouth of the Boyne, was the port of Drogheda, a place of painful memories for Catholics. For it was here, in 1649, that Oliver Cromwell had wreaked terrible vengeance, storming the town and slaughtering most of the garrison of some 3,000 men. Was James at all troubled by this ominous coincidence? Apparently not, since he chose to ignore the advice of his French officers, who for tactical reasons urged him to withdraw to more favourable terrain, and instead decided to stay put, come what may. 'He was resolved not to be tamely walked out of Ireland, but to have one blow for it at least.'[26]

In fact in military terms James was in quite a good position. The Boyne itself presented a natural obstacle for an advancing army, and there were high points in the undulating ground which would make good artillery platforms. On 30 June, whilst personally reconnoitring the situation with his staff including the ever-faithful Bentinck, William narrowly escaped a fate which could well have altered the outcome of the battle. A short, sudden bombardment from the southern banks not only showed that he had been recognised but almost succeeded in killing him. As it was, a ball or metal fragment grazed his shoulder, narrowly missing his chest and ripping away his coat and blood-stained shirt.[27] Apparently unperturbed by this escape, he made sure that by riding around amongst the lines (some say, on his conspicuous white horse) and showing himself to be uninjured there was no loss of morale amongst the troops, for the time was fast approaching when they would be tested to the full.

The moment finally arrived early on the morning of 1 July. A substantial body of William's troops, about 10,000 men under the overall command of Schomberg's son, Meinhardt, crossed the Boyne some 6 miles downriver from the village of Oldbridge. James, assuming this to be the advance guard of the rest of William's force, directed a large proportion of his own army, perhaps half of the total, to intercept it. He had been duped. At mid-morning William himself and the main body of his men forded the river at Oldbridge, in a determined onslaught headed by the Duke of Schomberg, who lost his life in the action. At first they met with strong resistance, but after about an hour enough of them had crossed the river to tip the balance in William's favour. For a time the Irish fought on, but eventually the superior training and discipline of William's men began to tell. With ever-gathering momentum, James' troops lost heart, threw down their weapons and left the field. A massacre of the retreating army was prevented only by the bravery of their cavalry and the disciplined rearguard action of the French regiments.[28] By the military standards of the times the number of lives lost was comparatively small. Irish losses amounted to about 1,500, William's army some 500.

At the start of the battle James had stationed himself at the rear of his army. While this is certainly not a sign of weakness in a commander (as exemplified by Wellington at Waterloo), James was nevertheless strategically well placed to make a quick exit from the field of battle, should this become necessary – as indeed it did. Once he saw that things were developing adversely for him, he lost no time in returning to Dublin and from there – pausing only to blame his soldiers for letting him down – going on to Duncannon in Waterford harbour, where he embarked for France on the armed merchantman *Lausanne* and was soon reunited with his family.[29] His reappearance, though welcome, was something of a surprise, for in Paris it had been widely reported that not only had James won the battle but also that William had been killed. Louis XIV was too polite to criticise his royal guest openly, but had probably already decided that no further French help would be forthcoming to help James regain his three kingdoms.[30] In 1696 he slightly changed his view and prepared to send troops in conjunction with an assassination plot against William hatched by a group of Jacobites. Headed by Sir George Barclay, a Scottish army officer, their plan was to abduct or kill the king in his coach as he passed through Turnham Green on his return from hunting – but two of the conspirators gave the game away and the rest were rounded up and mostly executed. Never again would James set foot in England, Scotland or Ireland.[31]

By 5 July William was securely established in Dublin. But after the Boyne he had been unusually slow in following up his advantages and had allowed much of the Jacobite army to slip away to Limerick, where it established a strong new base. In August an attempt to storm the city was repulsed with heavy losses to William's army, after which William himself returned to England, exasperated by the whole situation in Ireland and leaving behind the newly created Earl of Marlborough as his commander. Whilst still in Dublin he had received disturbing reports of a serious English-Dutch naval defeat by the French off Beachy Head on 30 June, the day before the Boyne. Unfortunately it was news of this disaster, rather than the successes in Ireland, which had grabbed the public's attention in London.

Although both Cork and Kinsale fell to Marlborough in the following weeks, their capture made little difference to the overall situation. As was customary, military activity petered out during the winter months; it revived in the spring of 1691 and built up to a crescendo which ended on 12 July with the Battle of Aughrim. This turned out to be a devastating and bloody defeat for the Irish, effectively signalling the end of the war. The death of Tyrconnell on 14 August (from natural causes) further strengthened William's resolve to bring an end to hostilities, and the fall of Limerick after a successful siege during August–September afforded an opportunity to put forward a treaty which it was hoped would stabilise events in Ireland.

The Treaty of Limerick was signed on 3 October 1691. Its main provisions not only affected the citizens of Limerick but also had a wider remit, in that Catholics throughout Ireland were promised such freedom to practise their religion as they had enjoyed under Charles II. It was further promised to the people of Limerick and other centres of resistance such as Kerry and Cork that their estates and property rights would be fully restored to them. The soldiery were given the option of remaining in Ireland or of going to France.

Following the Treaty the tumult in Ireland gradually subsided, the captains and the kings departed, and the exhausted populace picked its way wearily out of the ruins and bloodshed of the past years. When in 1697 the Irish Parliament – now almost entirely dominated by Protestants – shamefully ignored the Treaty and instead introduced new anti-Catholic measures, there was no longer any appetite for resistance. For the time being, the Irish dream was over.

AFTERMATH

With the suppression of the uprisings in Scotland and Ireland it seemed that the Revolution was complete. Declared 'Glorious' in its own day (although perhaps our modern view of it is rather less generous), there can be no doubt that many of those who lived through it and the years that followed were aware that significant political changes had taken place. Two such changes in particular stood out. First: limits to the powers of the monarch had begun to be clearly defined. There would no longer be much room for serious doubts as to what a reigning king or queen might or might not do without the sanction of Parliament. It is true that William himself continued to bypass Parliament in some crucial areas of policy, notably foreign affairs and the conduct of war. However, the 1701 Act of Settlement eventually brought these matters too into the spotlight of regular Parliamentary scrutiny.[1]

Second: despite a new and sometimes fragile climate of toleration towards religious Dissent (although Non-conformists were still barred from holding public office until 1828), Anglican Protestantism had been confirmed as the official religious basis of social and political life, and the royal Protestant succession was assured. Other, more obviously beneficial spin-offs included the final abolition of two especially contentious features of James II's reign – the use of the royal dispensing powers, and the maintenance of a standing army without Parliamentary consent. Moreover Parliament would meet regularly, not at the behest or whim of the reigning monarch. Within the narrower confines of Government the customary presence of the monarch at ministerial or Cabinet meetings soon fell into disuse. The position of judges was made secure; no longer could they be dismissed merely at the royal pleasure.

In financial matters, the monarch[s] would now receive an annual fixed sum which in any other walk of life would be called a salary but which in this case was called (and still is) the Civil List. Parliament, and not the king, would in future be responsible for defence spending.

With these reforms set firmly and finally in place by the Act of Settlement, it was perhaps reasonable to expect that the three kingdoms would settle down to a period of steady political development. But in the mid-1690s it was no more possible to foretell the future than we can do so today. English politics in fact became more divisive as the Whig and Tory parties took on their separate identities, and these divisions are still with us in one form or another. In 1707 Scotland lost its independence through the Act of Union and has only recently come any nearer to regaining it. Ireland endured a painful period of Protestant rule that eventually led to bloodshed and partition and to deep wounds whose scars are only now, it seems, slowly beginning to heal. Nevertheless setbacks, of whatever magnitude, should not blind us today to the achievements of the Revolution or cause us to deny its 'Glorious' credentials.

The return of some kind of stability to the three kingdoms meant that William could devote all his energies (plus – as he had always intended – additional manpower) to his consuming interest – the prosecution of the war against Louis XIV. The European background to the Glorious Revolution at home had been the onset in May 1689 of the so-called Nine Years War, curtain-raiser to the War of the Spanish Succession which would begin in 1701. During this period William suffered great personal loss through the death from smallpox of Queen Mary, on 28 December 1694. Her death was widely lamented. In the words of Bishop Burnet, 'Never was such a face of universal sorrow seen in a Court, or in a town, as at this time; all people … could scarcely refrain from tears.' None, however, grieved for her as much as her gruff husband who, despite an unpromising start to their marriage, had grown to love and respect her. Indeed the extent of William's grief was a surprise to his courtiers. To Burnet he confided 'that, from being the most happy, he was now going to be the most miserable creature upon the earth. He said [that] during the whole course of their marriage he had never known a single fault in her [and] that there was a worth in her that nobody knew besides himself.'[2] Today the unexpected intensity of her feelings for him is revealed in her letters. 'Love me, whatever happens, and be assured I am ever entirely yours till death ... With the hopes to see you, for which I am more impatient than can be expressed, loving you with a passion which cannot end but with my life.' So she had written to him in Ireland, before and after news of the Boyne had reached her.[3] For a time he seemed to go completely to pieces, but eventually he pulled himself together with the help of his closest friends and turned back to the thankless task of ruling alone.

The armies of William and Louis surged to and fro across Flanders in a series of inconclusive campaigns, to which the addition of newly available troops from England made little difference. There was, however, considerable difference in the cost to the country of men and materials which rose in these years from around £2 million to nearer £5 million. This phase of hostilities ended in 1697 with the Treaty of Ryswick. Not surprisingly, the beginning of the War of the Spanish Succession a mere four years later raised considerable apprehension in London, but preparations for the campaign nevertheless went ahead. Then, as so often in history, Fate took an unexpected hand.

On 21 February 1702 William was riding in Hyde Park when his horse stumbled over a molehill and he was thrown. His broken collarbone was repaired without difficulty and at first he seemed to be on the mend. However, symptoms of fever appeared on 5 March; the king gradually grew worse, and on 8 March he died. In contrast to that of his wife, his funeral in Westminster Abbey on 12 April was a private and subdued ceremony, as befitted a monarch who had never really captured the hearts of the people and to whom there are very few public memorials. 'The Prince of Orange [wrote Gilbert Burnet] was in his temper cold and reserved ... He had a gravity in his whole deportment, and a way that was affable and obliging to the Dutch; but he could not bring himself to comply enough with the temper of the English.'[4] William's successor was his sister-in-law Anne, whose death in 1714 finally brought the Stuart line to its end.

And what of James? Although there had been moments after 1690 when he had hoped that it might be possible once again to regain at least his English crown, those hopes were finally extinguished by two events. The first was the failure of the 1696 plot. The second was a clause in the 1697 Treaty of Ryswick specifically recognising William as the legitimate King of England. Even James now understood that he could never return, and he became resigned to his situation. His last years were spent in religious devotions which included fasting and self-mortification (but it seems did not exclude mistresses).[5] As his health deteriorated during the late 1690s he grew thin and gaunt, and early in 1701, after a stroke which temporarily paralysed his right side, he began to be subject to sudden fainting fits which weakened his already failing constitution. A final attack on 22 August signalled the end, which came on 5 September. During the French Revolution his tomb – in a Paris church – was desecrated and his corpse (minus some of the organs which had been removed at the time of death, including the heart) was exposed for a time to a gawping public before finally being unceremoniously disposed of.

Somehow this sadly unfitting and undignified end to a turbulent yet notable life sums up the contradictions inherent in James' character and actions. This was a monarch who above all wanted the English nation to return to full-blown Roman Catholicism, yet who also made religious tolerance one of the key elements of his policies. This was a king who, whilst having publicly promised at his accession 'to preserve the Government of the ... State as it is established by law', was nevertheless prepared to put himself above the law when it suited him. This was a commander who at a crucial moment changed from being a decisive and courageous leader of men into a feeble, dithering shadow of his former self. It is unlikely that modern historians will be any more successful than earlier ones have been in plumbing the depths of James' complex personality.

NOTES

Chapter 1

1   Extracts from Evelyn's *Diary*, as also from that of Samuel Pepys, are usually best found by referring to the actual dates cited, rather than by the use of distracting notes.

2   A. Fanshawe, *The Memoirs of Anne, Lady Fanshawe*, ed. H.C. Fanshawe, London 1907, pp. 24–5.

3   M. Ashley, *James II*, London 1977, p. 76.

4   *The Life of James the Second … collected out of memoirs writ by his own hand*, ed. J.S. Clarke, 2 vols, London 1816, vol. I, p. 401.

5   *Diary*, 6 September 1666.

6   G. Clark, *The Later Stuarts 1660–1714*, Oxford 1956, p. 68.

7   See *Life of James the Second*, vol. I, p. 471.

8   J. Burke, *An Illustrated History of England*, London 1974, p. 157.

9   B. Worden (ed.), *Stuart England*, Oxford, 1986, p. 169.

10 'The Orange and the Rose: Holland and Britain in the Age of Observation 1600–1750', catalogue of an Arts Council exhibition at the Victoria and Albert Museum, 22 October–13 December 1964, cat. no. 114, p. 52.

11 *Life of James the Second*, vol. I, p. 452.

12 Ashley, op. cit., p. 93.

13 Ibid. p. 91.

14 See especially the entry in Pepys' *Diary* for 23 June 1667.

15 G. Burnet, *Bishop Burnet's History of His Own Times*, abridged by T. Stackhouse, London 1906, p. 113.

16 *Life of James the Second*, vol. I, pp. 452–3; Ashley, op. cit., p. 93.

17 *Life of James the Second*, vol. I, p. 440.

18 See the article on James II in the *Oxford Dictionary of National Biography*, Oxford 2004.

19 A. Fraser, *King Charles II*, London 1979, p. 275; Ashley, op. cit., pp. 101–3.

20 Ashley, op. cit., p. 110.

21 *Life of James the Second*, vol. I, pp. 484–5.

22 In fact James was offered a choice between Mary and her 30-year-old aunt. He did not hesitate for long. See Fraser, op. cit., p. 322.

Chapter 2

1 Ashley, *James II*, p. 113.
2 Ibid. p. 114.
3 W. Troost, *William III, the Stadholder-King: A Political Biography*, trs. J.C. Grayson, Aldershot 2005, pp. 62–4.
4 Ibid.
5 Fraser, *King Charles II*, pp. 344, 347.
6 Ibid. pp. 348–9.
7 N. Murray, *World Enough and Time: The Life of Andrew Marvell*, London 1999, p. 246.
8 J. Pollock, *The Popish Plot: A Study in the History of the Reign of Charles II*, London 1903, pp. 4–5.
9 R. North, *The Lives of the Norths*, ed. A. Jessopp, 3 vols, London 1890, vol. I, p. 202.
10 Ibid. p. 201.
11 J. Millar, *Bourbon and Stuart: Kings and Kingship in France and England in the Seventeenth Century*, London 1987, p. 210.
12 North, op. cit., p. 216.
13 Ashley, op. cit., p. 122.
14 Fraser, op. cit., pp. 364–5.
15 North, op. cit., p. 211.
16 Fraser, op. cit., p. 379.
17 Ibid. p. 382.
18 Ibid. p. 387.
19 Ibid. p. 371.
20 Murray, op. cit., pp. 169–70; H. Chapman, *The Tragedy of Charles II in the Years 1630–1660*, London 1964, p. 331.
21 Ashley, op. cit., p. 128.
22 *Life of James the Second*, vol. I, p. 578.
23 Ibid. p. 132.
24 North, op. cit., p. 234.
25 C. Tomalin, *Samuel Pepys: The Unequalled Self*, London 2003, p. 331.
26 J. Lingard, *The History of England … to the Accession of William and Mary in 1688*, 5 edn, London 1848, vol. X, p. 102.
27 Ashley, op. cit., p. 150.

Chapter 3

1 Fraser, *King Charles II*, p. 453.
2 *Life of James the Second*, vol. I, p. 747.
3 Chapman, *The Tragedy of Charles II*, p. 198.
4 Ibid. p. 389.
5 Ibid. p. 390.
6 North, *Lives of the Norths*, vol. III, p. 177.
7 Ibid. vol. I, p. 332.

8   Ibid. vol. III, p. 177.
9   *Life of James the Second*, vol. II, p. 3.
10 Ibid. pp. 5–6.
11 James himself asserted that the funeral took place at night because of the conflict between the Anglican ceremony and the king's death-bed conversion. See *Life*, vol. II, pp. 6–7.
12 J. Aubrey, *Aubrey's Brief Lives*, ed. O.L. Dick, London 1972, p. 91.
13 A. Keay, *The Crown Jewels*, London 2011, pp. 101–7.
14 R. Strong, *Coronation: A History of Kingship and the British Monarchy*, London 2005, p. 347.
15 T. Harris, *Revolution: The Great Crisis of the British Monarchy 1685–1720*, London 2007, p. 55.
16 North, op. cit., vol. II, p. 209.
17 *Life of James the Second*, vol. II, p. 15.
18 Ibid. vol. I, p. 710.
19 North, op. cit., vol. I, pp. 336–9.
20 Lingard, *History of England*, pp. 203–4.
21 Ashley, op. cit., p. 159.
22 *A Compleat Collection of State Tryals ... for High Treason, and other Crimes and Misdemeanours; from the Reign of King Henry the Fourth to the End of the Reign of Queen Anne*, 4 vols, London 1719, vol. III, p. 48. See also Evelyn's *Diary* for 22 May 1685.
23 *Journals of the House of Commons* (afterwards cited as JHC), vol. IX, 1667–87, p. 715.
24 North, op. cit., vol. II, p. 210.
25 Lingard, op. cit., p. 164.
26 Harris, op. cit., pp. 75–6.
27 C. Barnett, *Marlborough*, London 1974, pp. 45–6.
28 Ashley, op. cit., p. 173.
29 North, op. cit., vol. I, p. 288.
30 Ibid.
31 See, for example, the trial of Alice Lisle in *State Tryals*, vol. III, pp. 492–514.
32 *Life of James the Second*, vol. II, p. 44.
33 *State Tryals*, pp. 655–6. This was in fact his second trial.
34 Harris, op. cit., pp. 90–5.
35 J. Childs, *The Army, James II, and the Glorious Revolution*, Manchester 1980, p. 126.
36 J.P. Kenyon, *The Stuarts*, London 1970, p. 130.
37 *Calendar of State Papers, Domestic Series, James II, Vol. III*, June 1687–February 1689 (afterwards cited as CSPD), London 1972, no. 532, p. 104.

Chapter 4

1   North, *Lives of the Norths*, vol. I, p. 352, vol. III, p. 194.
2   Ibid. vol. I, p. 253n.
3   Ibid. p. 269.
4   Ibid. pp. 270–1.
5   Barnett, *Marlborough*, p. 39.
6   Harris, *Revolution*, p. 175.

7   Childs, *The Army … and the Glorious Revolution*, p. 2.

8   North, op. cit., vol. I, pp. 358–9.

9   For these exchanges between king and Parliament, see the *Parliamentary History of England*, 36 vols, London 1806–20, vol. IV, p. 1,371; see also *The Life of James the Second*, vol. II, pp. 48–57.

10 Childs, op. cit., p. 97.

11 Ashley, *James II*, p. 192.

12 See Childs, op. cit., pp. 43–6.

13 *Parliamentary History*, vol. IV, p. 1,381.

14 Rougham Hall, Norfolk; North MS 23C1-5.

15 North, *Lives of the Norths*, vol. III, p. 179.

16 Harris, op. cit., p. 193.

17 Ibid. p. 199.

18 Ashley, op. cit., p. 157.

19 North, *Examen*, 1740, p. 77.

20 North, *Lives of the Norths*, vol. II, p. 229.

21 Harris, op. cit., p. 197.

22 Ibid. pp. 199–200.

23 *State Tryals*, p. 695.

24 *Life of James the Second*, vol. II, p. 91.

25 Ibid., vol. I, pp. 502–3.

26 G. Burnet, *History of His Own Times*, p. 245.

27 Harris, op. cit., p. 225.

28 CSPD no. 338, pp. 69–70; *Life of James the Second*, vol. II, pp. 119–25.

29 *State Tryals*, p. 742; see also continuation, *A Complete Collection of State Trials*, 33 vols, London 1809–28, vol. XII 1687–96, ed. T.B. Howell, London 1812, pp. 234–5.

30 North, *Lives of the Norths*, vol. III, p. 179.

31 See CSPD nos 27, 64, pp. 5, 12.

32 Harris, op. cit., p. 229.

33 CSPD no. 320, p. 66.

Chapter 5

1   North, *Lives of the Norths*, vol. III, pp. 121.

2   A. Strickland, *The Lives of the Seven Bishops*, London 1866, pp. 255–6, 258–60.

3   *State Trials* (1812), pp. 454–5.

4   Ibid. p. 461.

5   Ibid. p. 454.

6   Ibid. pp. 349–50.

7   Harris, *Revolution*, p. 265.

8   *State Trials* (1812), p. 430.

9   Harris, op. cit., p. 268.

10 Ashley, *James II*, p. 226.

11 *State Trials* (1812), p. 198.

12 CSPD no. 1236, pp. 223–4.

13 *State Trials* (1812), p. 130.

14 Ibid. p. 151.

15 CSPD no. 1177, p. 212.
16 Ashley, op. cit., p. 233; E. Vallance, *The Glorious Revolution 1688: Britain's Fight for Liberty*, London 2006, pp. 110–2.
17 Vallance, op. cit., p. 110.
18 CSPD no. 1346, p. 245.
19 Vallance, op. cit., pp. 111–2.
20 CSPD no. 1618, p. 298.
21 For an account of James' dealings with the bishops see *State Trials* (1812), pp. 488–91.
22 *Life of James the Second*, vol. II, p. 203; CSPD no. 1834, pp. 336–7.
23 *State Trials* (1812), p. 496.
24 JHC vol. X, 1688–93, pp. 1–4; CSPD no. 1665, p. 307; Harris, op. cit., pp. 279, 565.
25 Between 1684 and 1700 the future Queen Anne endured seventeen pregnancies, but only five of her children were born alive and none survived to adulthood.
26 *State Trials* (1812), pp. 123–42; CSPD no. 1774, p. 327; *Life of James the Second*, vol. II, pp. 198–203.
27 *State Trials* (1812), pp. 498, 506.
28 Harris, op. cit., pp. 279, 282.
29 CSPD no. 1131, p. 205.
30 Ibid. no. 1715, p. 316.
31 H. Ellis, *Original Letters Illustrative of English History*, series II, 4 vols, London 1827, vol. IV, p. 155.
32 CSPD no. 1346, p. 244.
33 Childs, *The Army ... and the Glorious Revolution*, p. 171.
34 Harris, op. cit., pp. 274–5.
35 CSPD no. 1346, p. 245.
36 For a full discussion of Burnet's status and influence, see T. Claydon, *William III and the Godly Revolution*, Cambridge 1996.
37 Burnet's *History* was one of John Keats' favourite books as a schoolboy. See A. Motion, *Keats*, London 1997, p. 38.
38 See *The Diary of Samuel Pepys*, ed. R. Latham, London 1983, vol. X (Companion), p. 208.
39 CSPD no. 1878, p. 343.
40 See M. Barone, *Our First Revolution: The Remarkable British Upheaval that Inspired America's Founding Fathers*, New York 2007, pp. 124–5.
41 CSPD no. 1549, p. 282.
42 Ibid. no. 1916, p. 348.
43 Burnet, *History of His Own Times*, p. 282.
44 *Life of James the Second*, vol. II, pp. 222–3.
45 CSPD no. 1983, p. 360.
46 Ashley, op. cit., p. 254.
47 CSPD no. 1986, p. 361.

Chapter 6

1   Ashley, *James II*, p. 254.
2   Burnet, *History of His Own Times*, p. 284; see also Barone, *Our First Revolution*, p. 164.
3   Vallance, *The Glorious Revolution*, p. 140.
4   CSPD no. 1965, p. 357.
5   Harris, *Revolution*, p. 285; Vallance, op. cit., p. 130; see also S. Pincus, *1688: The First Modern Revolution*, New Haven 2009, pp. 238–41.
6   *Life of James the Second*, vol. II, p. 231.
7   Ashley, op. cit., p. 257.
8   CSPD no. 2018, p. 367.
9   Vallance, op. cit., p. 143.
10 *Life of James the Second*, vol. II, pp. 233, 235–7; Ashley, op. cit., p. 256.
11 Tomalin, *Samuel Pepys*, p. 349.
12 Ibid.
13 CSPD no. 2087, pp. 377–8.
14 *Life of James the Second*, vol. II, pp. 256–8; Vallance, op. cit., p. 147.
15 Harris, op. cit., pp. 298–300.
16 See Burnet, op. cit., p. 309; Vallance, op. cit., p. 324 n. 11.
17 Harris, op. cit., p. 303; Vallance, op. cit., p. 145.
18 CSPD no. 2091, pp. 378–9; no. 2093, p. 380.
19 Ibid. no. 2094, p. 380.
20 *Life of James the Second*, vol. II, p. 259n.
21 Ibid. p. 263.
22 Ibid. p. 262–3; Vallance, op. cit., p. 157.
23 CSPD no. 2091, p. 379.
24 Barone, op. cit., p. 182.
25 *Life of James the Second*, vol. II, p. 266.
26 CSPD no. 2102, p. 382.
27 Ashley, op. cit., p 263; Vallance, op. cit., p. 160.
28 *Life of James the Second*, vol. II, p. 278.
29 JHC vol. X, p. 5.
30 Ibid. pp. 6, 7.
31 Lingard, *History of England*, p. 397.
32 Harris, op. cit., pp. 326–7.
33 Burnet, op. cit., p. 296.
34 Ibid.
35 Harris, op. cit., pp. 354–7.
36 M. Kishlansky, *A Monarchy Transformed: Britain 1603–1714*, London 1996, p. 286.
37 JHC vol. X, pp. 23–9.
38 Quoted in F. Molloy, *The Queen's Comrade: The Life of Sarah Duchess of Marlborough*, 2 vols, London 1901, vol. I, p. 137.
39 Burnet, op. cit., p. 250.
40 Keay, *The Crown Jewels*, pp. 111–3.
41 Strickland, *The Lives of the Seven Bishops*, pp. 78–9.
42 British Library Add. MS 32520.

Chapter 7

1 The will, with its signatories who also included George Jeffreys, is reproduced in *Life of James the Second*, vol. II, pp. 643–7.
2 Tomalin, *Samuel Pepys*, pp. 350–1.
3 Burnet, *History of His Own Times*, p. 292; Strickland, *The Lives of the Seven Bishops*, p. 85.
4 North, *Lives of the Norths*, vol. III, p. 113.
5 Harris, *Revolution*, p. 362.
6 Vallance, *The Glorious Revolution 1688*, p. 203.
7 Harris, op. cit., p. 392.
8 Vallance, op. cit., p. 204.
9 Harris, op. cit., p. 405.
10 See the article on Claverhouse in the Oxford DNB.
11 Harris, op. cit., p. 409.
12 Vallance, op. cit., p. 220.
13 Ibid. p. 223; *Life of James the Second*, vol. II, pp. 469–70 and n.
14 Harris, op. cit., p. 106.
15 Ibid. pp. 425–6; Vallance, op. cit., p. 210.
16 Vallance, op. cit., pp. 207–8.
17 Ibid. p. 209.
18 T.B. Macaulay, *The History of England*, 3 vols, London 1906, vol. II, p. 357.
19 Ibid. pp. 357–60.
20 Harris, op. cit., p. 443; Vallance, op. cit., pp. 212–3, 215.
21 Macaulay, op. cit., p. 394.
22 Vallance, op. cit., p. 216.
23 *Life of James the Second*, vol. II, p. 382.
24 Burnet, op. cit., pp. 322, 323.
25 Ibid., p. 323; Harris, op. cit., p. 446; Vallance, op. cit., p. 217.
26 *Life of James the Second*, vol. II, pp. 373, 377.
27 Vallance, op cit., p. 288.
28 *Life of James the Second*, vol. II, p. 401.
29 Ibid. pp. 404–6.
30 Macaulay, op. cit., pp. 702, 706.
31 Burnet, op. cit., pp. 371–4.

Chapter 8

1 Worden (ed.), *Stuart England*, pp. 205–6.
2 Burnet, *History of His Own Times*, pp. 359–60.
3 Strickland, A., *Lives of the Queens of England*, 12 vols, London 1844–48, vol. XI, pp. 76, 103.
4 Burnet, op. cit., p. 250.
5 Vallance, *The Glorious Revolution*, p. 296.

SELECT BIBLIOGRAPHY

Ashley, M., *James II*, London 1977.

Aubrey, J., *Aubrey's Brief Lives*, ed. O.L. Dick, London 1972.

Barone, M., *Our First Revolution: The Remarkable British Upheaval that Inspired America's Founding Fathers*, New York 2007.

Batey, M. and Woudstra, J., *The Story of the Privy Garden at Hampton Court*, Barn Elms 1995.

Baxter, S.B., *William III*, London 1966.

Bevan, B., *King William III, Prince of Orange, the First European*, London 1997.

Brome, V., *The Other Pepys*, London 1992.

Burke, J., *An Illustrated History of England*, London 1974.

Burnet, G., *Bishop Burnet's History of His Own Times*, abridged by T. Stackhouse, London 1906.

Calendar of State Papers, Domestic Series, James II, Volume III, June 1687–February 1689, London 1972.

Chapman, H., *The Tragedy of Charles II in the Years 1630–1660*, London 1964.

Childs, J., *The Army, James II, and the Glorious Revolution*, Manchester 1980.

Clark, G., *The Later Stuarts 1660–1714* (vol. X of *The Oxford History of England*), 2 edn, Oxford 1956.

Claydon, T., *William III and the Godly Revolution*, Cambridge 1996.

A Compleat Collection of State Tryals … for High Treason, and other Crimes and Misdemeanours, from the Reign of King Henry the Fourth to the End of the Reign of Queen Anne, 4 vols, London 1719; continued as *A Complete Collection of State Trials*, 33 vols, London 1809–28.

The Diary of John Evelyn, ed. E.S. de Beer, 6 vols, Oxford 1955.

The Diary of Samuel Pepys, ed. R. Latham and W. Matthews, 10 vols [incl. Companion], London 1970–83.

Fraser, A., *King Charles II*, London 1979.

Gibson, W., *James II and the Trial of the Seven Bishops*, Basingstoke 2009.

Ellis, H., *Original Letters Illustrative of English History*, 4 vols, London 1827.

Harris, T., *Revolution: The Great Crisis of the British Monarchy, 1685–1720*, London 2007.

Hoppit, J., *A Land of Liberty? England, 1727–1783* (*New Oxford History of England*), Oxford 2000.

Journals of the House of Commons, vols 1–56, London 1805–13.

Keay, A., *The Crown Jewels*, London 2011.

Kenyon, J.P., *The Stuarts: A Study in English Kingship*, London 1966.

Kishlansky, M., *A Monarchy Transformed: Britain 1603–1714*, London 1996.

The Life of James the Second ... collected out of memoirs writ by his own hand, ed. J.S. Clarke, 2 vols, London 1816.

Lingard, J., *The History of England ... to the Accession of William and Mary in 1688*, 5 edn, 10 vols, 1849.

Macaulay, T.B., *The History of England from the Accession of James II*, 3 vols, London 1906.

Millar, J., *Bourbon and Stuart: Kings and Kingship in France and England in the Seventeenth Century*, London 1987.

North, R., *The Lives of the Norths*, ed. A. Jessopp, 3 vols, London 1890.

North, R., *Examen: Or, an Enquiry into the Credit and Veracity of a Pretended Complete History, Shewing the Perverse and Wicked Design of It*, London, 1740.

Oman, C., *Mary of Modena*, London 1962.

The Orange and the Rose: Holland and Britain in the Age of Observation 1600–1750, catalogue of an Arts Council exhibition at the Victoria and Albert Museum, 22 October–13 December 1964.

Pincus, S., *1688: The First Modern Revolution*, New Haven 2009.

Pollock, J., *The Popish Plot: A Study in the History of the Reign of Charles II*, London 1903.

Seymour, W., *Battles in Britain and Their Political Background*, 2 vols, London 1975.

Speck, W.A., *Reluctant Revolutionaries*, Oxford 1988.

Starkey, D., *Crown and Country: A History of England Through the Monarchy*, London 2006.

Strickland, A., *Lives of the Queens of England*, 12 vols, London 1844–48.

Strickland, A., *The Lives of the Seven Bishops*, London 1866.

Strong, R., *Coronation: A History of Kingship and the British Monarchy*, London 2005.

Sturgis, M., *Hampton Court Palace*, London 1998.

Tomalin, C., *Samuel Pepys: The Unequalled Self*, London 2003.

Trevelyan, G.M., *English Social History: A Survey of Six Centuries, Chaucer to Queen Victoria*, London 1948.

Troost, W., *William III, the Stadholder-King: A Political Biography*, trs. J.C. Grayson, Aldershot 2005.

Uglow, J., *A Gambling Man: Charles II and the Restoration 1660–1670*, London 2009.

Vallance, E., *The Glorious Revolution 1688: Britain's Fight for Liberty*, London 2006.

Waller, M., *1700: Scenes from London Life*, London 2000.

Worden, B. (ed.), *Stuart England*, Oxford 1986.

INDEX

Titles and other modes of address given here are mainly those that were in use up to and during the years of the Revolution and its immediate aftermath.

If you enjoyed this book, you may also be interested in …

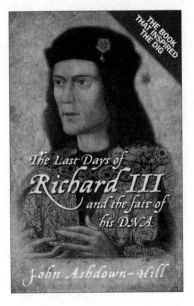

The Last Days of Richard III

JOHN ASHDOWN-HILL

978 0 7524 9205 6

The Last Days of Richard III contains a new and uniquely detailed exploration of Richard's last 150 days. It re-examines the aftermath of Bosworth: the treatment of Richard's body; his burial; and the construction of his tomb. And there is the fascinating story of why, and how, Richard III's family tree was traced until a relative was found, alive and well, in Canada. Now, with the discovery of Richard's skeleton at the Greyfrairs Priory in Leicester, England, John Ashdown-Hill explains how his book inspired the dig and completes Richard III's fascinating story, giving details of how Richard died, and how the DNA link to a living relative of the king allowed the royal body to be identified.